HOW T
CASTLES

HOW TO READ
CASTLES

A crash course in understanding fortifications

B L O O M S B U R Y
LONDON · NEW DELHI · NEW YORK · SYDNEY

Malcolm Hislop

First published in Great Britain in 2013 by
Bloomsbury Publishing plc
50 Bedford Square
London WC1B 3DP, UK
www.bloomsbury.com

ISBN: 978-1-4725-2161-3
2012 2013 2014 2015
10 9 8 7 6 5 4 3 2 1

A CIP catalogue record for this book
is available from the British Library

Colour origination by Ivy Press
Reprographics

Printed in China

This book was conceived,
designed and produced by
Ivy Press
210 High Street
Lewes, East Sussex
BN7 2NS, UK
www.ivypress.co.uk

CREATIVE DIRECTOR Peter Bridgewater
PUBLISHER Jason Hook
EDITORIAL DIRECTOR Caroline Earle
ART DIRECTOR Michael Whitehead
SENIOR EDITOR Stephanie Evans
DESIGN JC Lanaway

Contents

They are gaunt relics of obsolete societies, yet castles raise in us a frisson of excitement as we spy their dilapidated yet dignified remains rising above the surrounding landscape. To the casual observer, one castle may seem much like another, their earthworks, high walls, towers and narrow openings evoking the grimness of a harsher, less secure age. There is, of course, a generic relationship between all these sites, but it is worth stressing that castles were built for over 600 years in Europe (c.900–c.1500), and underwent considerable change, both generally, as concepts of design and construction evolved, and as individual buildings as they were adapted to the needs of successive generations.

The purpose of this handbook is to provide a framework for the visitor, so that each castle might be interpreted and placed in context. What was its purpose? How was it built? How did it work? The first part of the book gives a broad outline of the subject, with sections on function, design and

Calahorra Tower
The Calahorra Tower in Cordoba, Spain, was built in the 12th century in the Islamic style as a gateway to the city. The building was converted into a great tower in the 14th century.

construction and castle types. The second part is an exposition of the features that make up a castle.

In interpreting a castle, bear in mind two aspects: site and structure. Many castle sites were chosen with a view to facilitating defence and observation of the surroundings, which accounts for the many examples that occupy elevated positions. Such locations gave tactical benefits, but a castle's purpose was often strategic as well, and taking note of its situation in respect of the distribution of population, the communications network and agricultural production will provide clues to its purpose.

While some castles were instruments of conquest, others were the residential and administrative centres of landed estates and had a largely peaceful intent. The character of a castle's structures will suggest whether its prime function was that of a fortress, or whether it had a more domestic role. Was a tower residential or was it intended as a base for archers and crossbowmen? Does the character of a window have anything to tell us about the function of a room and the approach to defence? Noting the physical evidence will allow us to draw conclusions to questions such as these.

Bamburgh Castle
Bamburgh Castle in Northumberland is a multi-period site, dramatically positioned on a rocky coastal headland. The location was chosen for the quality of its natural defences.

Looking for Clues

Contrasting designs
Château de Falaise
in Normandy, France,
retains a cuboid great
tower built in the 1120s
by Henry I, King of
England and Duke
of Normandy. To the
right of Henry's tower,
quite different in style
and clearly of a different
date, is the cylindrical
Talbot Tower, which was
raised in the early years
of the 13th century by
Philip II Augustus, King
of France, after he had
captured the castle. The
divergent characters
of these two towers
indicate that there
were at least two
important building
periods at Falaise.

While some castles were built in a single recognisable
phase, most have undergone centuries of adaptation,
and are amalgamations of several building periods.
Historical evidence is often limited in what it can
tell us about the sequence of a castle's development,
and it is usually by analysing clues within the fabric
of the building itself that a more detailed structural
history can be compiled. Architectural details, structural
anomalies and planning concepts all provide evidence
for interpretation.

Evidence of lost buildings

Anomalies in the stonework sometimes indicate the former existence of attached structures. At Scarborough Castle in Yorkshire, wall stubs protruding from the face of the mid-12th-century great tower to either side of the entrance demonstrate that the entrance was originally contained within a defensive forebuilding that has since been demolished.

Remodelled structures

In updating accommodation, masons often incorporated fragments of earlier buildings into new structures, and these can be used to trace the history of a castle. One example is the survival of a 12th-century blocked fireplace in the great hall of Warkworth Castle, in Northumberland, which was partially rebuilt in the 15th century.

Masonry techniques

Different building phases can often be identified by the contrasting qualities of the stonework. The curtain wall of Alnwick Castle, in Northumberland, displays evidence of at least two distinct building periods distinguished by different masonry techniques. The 12th-century work seen on the right, which consists of coursed and squared stone blocks, contrasts markedly with the later masonry to the left and the rebuilt battlements and turret above.

The Grammar of Castles

Introduction

Castles had two main functions. On the one hand they were fortifications with both defensive and offensive aspects; on the other, they were aristocratic residences, particularly associated with the knightly class. This combination of martial and residential roles governed the architectural nature of the castle and distinguished it from other forms of building. While both facets were always present, their relative significance varied to the extent that one castle might be predominantly military in nature and another mainly domestic. Determining the precise function of a castle is one of the most satisfying tasks of the investigator.

Arques-la-Bataille

The hilltop château of Arques-la-Bataille near Dieppe in Normandy, France, is 11th century in origin, shown here in its possible 12th-century form. Its defensive aspect is the enceinte: a palisaded bank, ditch, and stone curtain with interval towers. In contrast, the domestic buildings within make no concession to defence. The exception is the great tower, which had both domestic and defensive capacity.

A contemporary view

The dichotomous nature of the castle is illustrated in this drawing from a medieval manuscript. It shows a crenellated curtain wall, projecting towers and a prominent gatehouse defended by a portcullis. Within this fortification is a large domestic building with tall windows and a chimney. The two elements – domesticity and defence – appear to have been accorded equal significance.

Bellver Castle

An example of a castle where domestic and defensive elements form an integrated architectural conception is Bellver Castle near Palma on the island of Mallorca. At Bellver the ditched outer walls of the castle are lined with apartments to enclose a courtyard. It is evident that the structure has been designed as a single entity.

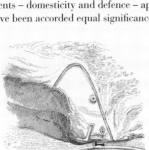

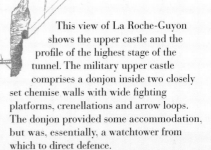

Château de La Roche-Guyon (above and right)

La Roche-Guyon, in northern France, has two distinct elements. Its residential apartments (15th century) are by the river at the cliff foot. At the cliff top, connected to the lower castle by a tunnel, is a late-12th-century castle of overtly military character. This construction, intended to protect the lower castle, is set in a ditched enclosure.

This view of La Roche-Guyon shows the upper castle and the profile of the highest stage of the tunnel. The military upper castle comprises a donjon inside two closely set chemise walls with wide fighting platforms, crenellations and arrow loops. The donjon provided some accommodation, but was, essentially, a watchtower from which to direct defence.

Norman Expansion

Castle building proliferated in the 11th century through the military adventures of the Normans, the inhabitants of the politically obscure duchy of Normandy in northern France. The Normans are probably best known for their conquest of England in 1066, under Duke William, when his invading army disembarked at Pevensey on the Sussex coast. The Bayeux Tapestry vividly illustrated their conquest of England, although by this time Norman adventurers had already carved out states for themselves in southern Italy and were to go on to establish the kingdom of Sicily, which included the southern half of the Italian peninsula. From Italy a Norman contingent set out for the First Crusade, and went on to set up a principality based on the city of Antioch.

The White Tower

The Tower of London was one of the early fortresses established by William in the wake of the Conquest. Set within a corner of the Roman city walls, it was the site of the White Tower, the secular architectural masterpiece of the age. Probably begun in the 1070s and completed by 1100, the White Tower was a fortress in its own right, but it also contained a palatial residence and was a strident expression of political power.

La Cuba

In the early 12th century, the Normans established the kingdom of Sicily, a rich cosmopolitan state in which Norman, Greek and Muslim influences mingled. La Cuba, built for William II, King of Sicily, c.1180, is rectangular in plan with square turrets breaking forward from three sides. The design is that of a Norman keep, but the blind arcading on the outer walls, and the interior decoration, are probably by Muslim workmen.

Antioch

Captured from the Turks by the invading crusader army in 1098, the ancient city of Antioch, now in southern Turkey, formed the centre of a Christian principality founded by Bohemond I, scion of an Italian Norman dynasty, during the First Crusade. The Byzantines fortified the city in the 6th century and restored the defences in the late 10th century. In the 1090s these fortifications presented a formidable obstacle to the Crusaders and it was only through treachery that the city was taken.

Crusades

Krak des Chevaliers
Krak des Chevaliers in Syria, built between 1142 and 1170 as an enclosure castle with rectangular wall towers, is exceptionally well defended. In the early 13th century it was enlarged by enclosing the 12th-century core with a new outer circuit incorporating rounded wall towers. The result was a castle greatly strengthened through having an outer circuit commanded by an inner circuit.

The First Crusade, which set out in 1096 to invade, capture and maintain the Holy Land for Christendom, resulted in the establishment of a number of autonomous states. Castles were the key to retaining the captured lands and they provided a stimulus to the architectural development of the castle in the Middle East and Europe. As these fortress castles changed hands frequently, they display Muslim and Byzantine as well as European characteristics. Many of them were held by the military orders, organisations of monks formed to protect pilgrims to the Holy Land, the principal ones being the Templars and the Hospitallers, and later the Teutonic Knights.

Margat Castle

Built on a Syrian hill overlooking the Mediterranean, Margat was in the hands of the Hospitallers by 1186. Its defences, which enclose a town as well as the castle or citadel, were strengthened in the 13th century. The castle has a rounded donjon at its southern apex, which is incorporated into the curtain. The walls tower above and dominate the outer defences.

Saone Castle

Held by Muslims in the 10th century, and by Byzantines after 975, Saone, in Syria, was captured by the Crusaders in the early 12th century and remained in their hands until Saladin took it in 1188. The castle and associated town occupy a spur, which the Crusaders isolated by excavating a massive ditch across its eastern end. The main defensive work, shown here, incorporates both rectangular residential towers, and round turrets primarily military in function.

Kolossi Castle

Richard the Lionheart's conquest of Cyprus in 1191, during the Third Crusade, brought the island into the sphere of the Crusader states. The kingdom of Cyprus survived long after the mainland states fell into the hands of the Muslims, and it was to Cyprus that the military orders moved their headquarters. The Knights Hospitaller were granted Kolossi Castle in 1212. Its main feature is the rectangular great tower of c.1460, a self-contained building with water cistern, kitchen, storerooms and the lodgings of the Grand Commander.

Warfare in Europe

Ponferrada Castle
Ponferrada, sited at the confluence of the rivers Boeza and Sil in the former kingdom of León in Spain, lay on the route of Christian pilgrims visiting Santiago de Compostela. A bridge was built over the Sil in the late 11th century, and the castle, set on a hill overlooking the river and bridge, was probably sited to protect this route. In the late 12th century it was granted to the Knights Templar.

Just as a constant readiness for war was an abiding feature of the Crusader states, so was warfare also a continual presence in parts of Europe, often initiated by religious differences. On the Iberian peninsula, the Christian states' reconquest of the areas under Muslim occupation lasted from the 8th to the 15th century. In north-eastern Europe, following the demise of the Crusader states in the Holy Land, the Teutonic Knights concentrated their efforts on the conquest of the heathen lands bordering the Baltic, and in so doing carved out a powerful Christian state. In both these areas castles were essential weapons in maintaining a grip on conquered territory, as shown in the illustrated examples given here.

Ávila

The fortifications of Ávila, in Spain, were raised by Raymond of Burgundy shortly after the capture of Toledo from the Muslims in 1085. As a fortified city, its initial role may have been to provide a defendable base where troops could gather in safety. The rounded towers are an unusually early example of this form.

San Servando Castle

Sited on the east side of the River Tagus, opposite the city of Toledo, Spain, the castle of San Servando overlooks the Alcántara Bridge, which gave it great strategic importance. Originally a monastery, it was reconstructed in the 1380s by Archbishop Pedro Tenorio to guard the eastern river crossing into the city.

Malbork Castle

The castle of Malbork, in northern Poland, was the headquarters of the Teutonic Knights from the early 14th century until 1457. Behind the waterfront buildings the Upper Castle (on the right), 1276–c.1300, contained the main living quarters, whereas the Middle Castle (on the left), c.1310–50, contained guest accommodation.

Hall of the Knights: Malbork Castle

As a castle of the Teutonic Knights, Malbork was also a monastery and as such, hospitality was one of its functions. The Hall of the Knights, which was built on a grand scale in a highly decorative fashion between 1318 and c.1340, was the refectory for guests and visiting members of the Order.

Expansion of Russia

Moscow Kremlin
Founded in the 11th
century, the Moscow
kremlin occupies an
elevated position on the
north bank of the River
Moskva. The red brick
walls were built by
Italian architects, from
1485–95, for Ivan III,
Grand Prince of Moscow,
shortly after Muscovy
freed itself from
Mongol suzerainty.

On the eastern periphery of Europe were the Slavic principalities whose former territories now fall within the Russian Federation. The origins of Russian castles can probably be traced to the breakdown of the early medieval state of Kievan Rus' into feudal principalities, and the resulting proliferation of minor lordships. Like their more westerly European counterparts, these lordly castles sometimes precipitated the growth of a town, of which they became the citadel or kremlin. As Muscovy threw off the overlordship of the Mongols in the late 15th century and began to expand, kremlins played their part in consolidating the enlarged territories.

Red Square

St Basil

(A) Nicholas Gate
(B) Redeemer Gate
(C) Postern
(D) Forest Gate
(E) Trinity Gate
(F) Convent
(G) Monastery
(H) Nicholas Palace
(I) Bell Tower
(J) Great Bell
(K) Cath. of the Archangel
(L) Cath. of the Annunciation
(M) Grand Palace
(N) Cath. of the Assumption
(O) St. Constantine

Moscow Kremlin (plan)

The walls enclose an irregular
triangular space with the
Moskva to the south and its
tributary stream, the Neglinnaya,
to the west. The main gateway
from the city lies within the
east side. The kremlin contains
two palaces, three cathedrals, a
monastery and a convent, along
with administrative buildings
and barracks.

Kazan Kremlin

Topping a hill beneath which the Volga and
Kazanka rivers meet, Kazan's kremlin is on
the site of a 12th-century fortress destroyed
by the Mongols, and later redeveloped as
the citadel of the Muslim Kazan khanate.
Kazan was conquered by the Russians in
1552, and its kremlin was rebuilt with a
mixture of round and rectangular towers.

Nizhny Novgorod Kremlin

Nizhny Novgorod kremlin is located on a
highly strategic point at the meeting of the
Volga and Oka rivers. As this view of the
kremlin from across the Volga shows, in
addition to having a good strategic position,
it occupies a tactically advantageous site
on a hill overlooking the confluence.

Warfare in Japan

Osaka Castle
Osaka is built in the Yodo delta on artificial platforms. A large outer courtyard surrounds an inner courtyard housing the lord's apartments, including a great tower. Four gateways, each approached by a bridge, give access to the outer courtyard. The inner courtyard has only two entrances. The castle's strength lay in the steeply battered stone revetment walls and deep water-filled moats.

While castles are principally associated with European culture, comparable structures were found in other parts of the medieval and later world. In Japan there was a society that produced similar conditions to those of feudal Europe, and in which the castle flourished. Japanese castles provide an interesting parallel with those of Europe, since they display a degree of similiarity through the application of shared concepts, but nevertheless represent a quite separate architectural tradition. The unsettled Sengoku period (1467–1603) provided a great impetus to castle building. Many of the classic Japanese castles, including Osaka and Nagoya, date from the 16th and 17th centuries when the great tower (*tenshukaku*) became a recurrent feature.

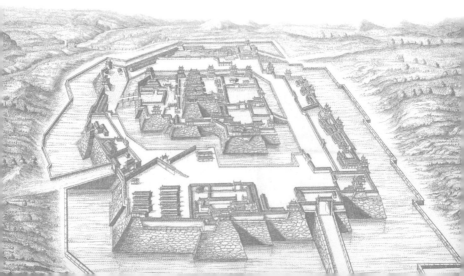

Nagoya Castle

Nagoya Castle was rebuilt by the shogun Tokugawa Ieyasu, as the new administrative centre of Owari province. The great tower formed part of the private quarters of the castle's lord. As such it was an entirely domestic building rather than being associated with defence.

Edo Castle

Edo was one of the most politically significant of Japanese castles. It became the seat of the shogun and later the Imperial Palace. It was a vast complex enclosed by a series of moats and walls, with the domestic accommodation disposed in a carefully regulated hierarchy.

Kasugayama Castle

Many early Japanese castles used natural features and topography to enhance their fortification. Kasugayama is a *yamashiro*, where the mountain has been terraced into a sequence of baileys, one above another, leading up to the inner courtyard in which the lord's apartments are found.

Gassan Toda Castle

Prominent at Gassan Toda is the use of sloping stone revetments to the sides of the bailey platforms and the bases of some buildings (including the great tower). The sloping character of such revetments recalls *yamashiro* in which the shape of the mountain is reflected in the design of the masonry.

Communications

The strategic purpose of many castles was to control an important route of communication, either a road or a waterway. This might be for military purposes or to exact dues from travellers. Military purposes governed the thinking of strategists in the Crusader states after 1187, when they were reduced to a narrow coastal strip of the Holy Land highly vulnerable to Muslim powers to the east. A favoured site for a castle was at a river crossing where the construction of a bridge, or the operation of a ferry, gave an opportunity to charge tolls. A navigable waterway like the Rhine formed a major artery of communication from which an income might be derived by the lords of the adjacent lands.

The toll station
Many of the castles along the River Rhine in Germany were positioned with a view to extracting tolls from the users of this important waterway. Pfalzgrafenstein, established by King Ludwig the Bavarian in 1327, was built on an island in the river, making it eminently suited to its function.

The river crossing

Rochester Castle, in Kent, was founded soon after the Norman conquest. It lay on the main route between London and Canterbury, part of the former Roman road known as Watling Street. Its strategic purpose was to control the crossing over the River Medway. The curtain wall was rebuilt in the 1080s and the great tower was raised in the early 12th century.

The regional crossroads

The castle at Tutbury, on the Staffordshire/Derbyshire border, was built by Hugh D'Avranches c.1068–69. Situated on a commanding hill overlooking the River Dove, its strategic purpose was to provide a base from which both north–south and east–west lines of communication within the region could be controlled.

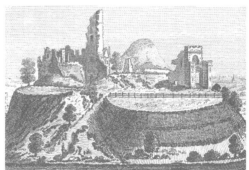

The coastal road

Chastel Pelerin at Athlit, in the former kingdom of Jerusalem, was built in 1218 to protect the road between Caesarea and Acre. Sited on a coastal promontory cut off from the mainland by the excavation of a great ditch across its neck, the castle had a harbour and so could be victualled and relieved by sea. It was held by the Templars until the demise of the kingdom near the end of the 13th century.

Early Siege Warfare

Dinan Castle

The Bayeux Tapestry records William of Normandy's attack on Dinan, in Brittany, France, c.1064. The castle is depicted as a banked and ditched motte surmounted by a palisade and tower. The assault is depicted largely as a conventional battle of opposing forces armed with spears.

The evolution of castle architecture in the 12th and 13th centuries was, to a great extent, bound up with improvements in siege warfare techniques. While the timber defences of many early castles may not seem so intimidating, they offered a very distinct advantage to the defenders over enemies unversed in siege tactics. As the castle's role in warfare strengthened, military engineers directed their minds towards overcoming the obstacles they presented; and as siege techniques became more effective, defences needed to become more formidable.

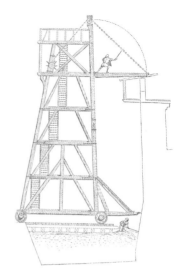

The belfry in use

Several storeys high, and capable of holding large numbers of men, these machines rose above a castle's curtain wall, enabling the besieging army to fire missiles down into the castle. Preparation for an assault by belfry involved filling and levelling any ditch around the castle.

The belfry (cross-section)

Belfries were timber-framed constructions set on wheels – mobile siege towers similar to the static towers of timber castles. A drawbridge near the top allowed armed men to access the battlements of the enemy's castle.

The ram

The ram was a weapon of ancient origin used to break down wooden gates and doors. Originally a simple device dependent on muscle power, it became far more effective when harnessed to a carpentry frame. Suspension from the frame meant that the ram could be swung repeatedly against the obstacle with far greater impetus and force and with economy of effort. The end of the ram was reinforced with an iron cap to prevent it splintering.

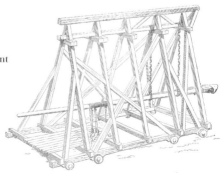

Bombardment & Mining

The mangonel
The mangonel was a giant catapult. At one end a wooden arm was placed between a skein of ropes stretching from one side of the mangonel frame to the other. The ropes were wound tight and the arm kept in an upright position by a horizontal bar. The cup at the free end of the arm was then pulled down, secured and loaded. Releasing the cup flicked it back into position, hurling the missile towards its target.

The medieval military engineer had a number of artillery weapons at his disposal that he could use to weaken the besieged fortress by keeping up a constant bombardment. Through this he could inflict both physical and psychological harm. Most effective were the great stone-throwing devices, known by the collective term *petrarie*, which could attack the fabric of the castle as well as its inhabitants. In addition to dispatching rocks, they might be used to throw dead animals and other disgusting burdens into the castle in order to spread disease and to demoralise. A quite different, but nevertheless widely used and effective tactic, was the excavation of tunnels to undermine the defences and afford access to the castle.

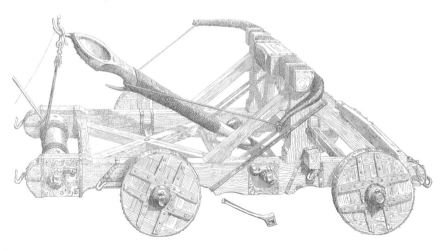

Mining

One of the most feared and effective methods of siege warfare was tunnelling under the fortification. Because mining was an underground operation it could often be kept secret from the defenders, giving the besiegers the advantage of surprise. Tunnelling brought down the corner of the keep of Rochester, in Kent, during the siege of 1215.

The trebuchet

During the 12th century a new machine that worked on the principle of counterweight was developed. The mechanics were simpler and the machines more reliable than mangonels, but trebuchets were considerably larger, and therefore less mobile. They also required a greater investment.

Preparing the trebuchet

This illustration of a trebuchet is from *The Portfolio of Villard de Honnecourt*, c.1230. Attached to the right-hand end of the pivoted great beam is a sling, charged with a missile and placed between the two beam supports. At the left-hand end of the beam is a box filled with stones or other heavy material, raised and ready to be released.

Architectural Responses

Improvements in siege warfare engendered a reaction among castle builders, resulting in a more scientific approach to defence. Wall towers, which in early castles were placed sporadically, were now deployed in a more methodical fashion in order to maximise control over the curtain. Rectangular towers gave way to rounded ones, which were less vulnerable to mining, more able to deflect missiles, and better suited to the creation of a more comprehensive field of fire through the use of arrow loops. Improvements to the defences of some castles were directly related to the experience of being under attack, but most defensive systems were more theoretical, and might never be put to the test.

Château Gaillard

Château Gaillard, in Normandy, France, is in a superb tactical position, and was one of the most considered pieces of military architecture of the age. Built by Richard the Lionheart between 1196 and 1198, it sits on a spur some 91.5 m (300 ft) above the River Seine. It was the work of a highly experienced and proactive soldier familiar with siege warfare. There is little doubt of its military character – it was designed for the purpose of countering an attack.

Deflective design: La Roche-Guyon (plan)
Château Gaillard was probably influenced by La Roche-Guyon, built c.1190 on a cliff above the Seine. The beaked donjon and two lines of concentric defences are streamlined, possibly to maximise their deflective qualities and present a difficult target for the petrarie operators.

Donjon: La Roche-Guyon
The beaked donjon and curtain provided prows of immense thickness and strength, and minimised the possibility of a direct hit by a stone-throwing engine. The double curtain in front of the donjon foreshadowed the development of concentric fortifications that occurred in the following century.

Bailey wall: Château Gaillard
One of the most innovative features of Château Gaillard was its inner bailey wall, which included a series of rounded projections. These features strengthened the wall and broke up its surface, which increased its ability to deflect missiles and allowed a greater field of fire.

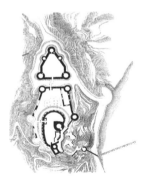

Defence sequence: Château Gaillard (plan)
Gaillard has natural defences on three sides, including a precipitous cliff above the river. The one open approach was defended by a ditch cut across the neck of the spur and a sequence of three baileys, connected with staggered gateways. In the outer bailey, a keep with a beaked front faced the approach.

Impact of Artillery

The development of artillery in the later Middle Ages led to a response in the design of castles. Cannon were in use by the early 14th century, but as small-calibre anti-personnel weapons, they had little effect on castle architecture other than to prompt the appearance of gun loops in otherwise traditional castles. As the calibre of guns increased, so did their destructive capacity, and by the 15th century outworks or 'bulwarks' were being thrown up around older defences to combat the threat. The builders of new fortifications began to take cannon into account in formulating their designs for defence and for returning fire to the enemy.

Cannon power

This illustration of the 1641 Spanish siege of Hohentwiel, in Baden-Württemberg, southern Germany, emphasises that the development of artillery posed a much greater threat to castles than any of the methods of medieval siege warfare. Cannon power surpassed medieval siege engines in its greater range and destructive capability, and could therefore be used to 'soften up' the target by inflicting real damage from a safe distance.

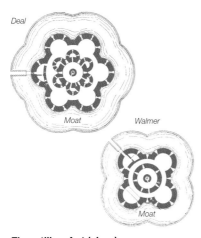

Deal

Moat

Walmer

Moat

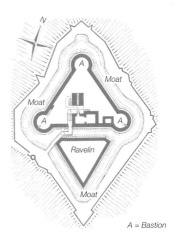

N

A

Moat

Moat

A

A

Ravelin

Moat

A = Bastion

The artillery fort (plans)

Henry VIII's break with Rome prompted the construction of coastal artillery forts from 1539–43. These were compact and squat, with several tiers of concentrated firepower. Deal and Walmer, in Kent, are typical: geometric in plan, with bastions for large gun emplacements based on the circle. Defences are concentric, with taller central cores overlooking outer defences. Deal could deploy four tiers of guns.

The angle bastion (plan)

Designed for Lorenzo de' Medici c.1493, Castello di Sarzanello, in northern Italy, is an early example of a fort designed with angle bastions to accommodate artillery. Built to a plan based on the equilateral triangle, it has a round bastion at each corner to facilitate flanking fire across the curtain. A slightly later outwork to the south, also triangular, is the earliest example of a ravelin, a device designed to break up the thrust of an assault.

Adaptation: Château Bonaguil

Bonaguil, in south-west France, adapted to the age of gunpowder by reorganising its defences. The 13th-century castle was remodelled and extended in the late 1400s and early 1500s. The donjon, rebuilt as a tapering polygon, formed the east side of the inner courtyard, and corner towers were added to the east and west. Around this core a second, low curtain was built with bastions, gun loops and an artillery platform.

Royal Palace

Windsor Castle
Founded by William the Conqueror c.1070, Windsor Castle had become the main residence of the English monarchs by the end of the century. During its great transformation, carried out 1350–68 by Edward III, the royal lodgings in the upper bailey were improved and the 12th-century shell keep on the motte was remodelled as a courtyard house.

Royal castles, important as fortresses, also contained the private dwellings of the monarch. As such they had the potential to become favoured residences and to be developed in palatial fashion. In some cases the location of such residences was down to political expedients, but in others it was the recreational facilities offered by a site that was probably the principal factor. Several royal castles with their origins in the Middle Ages retained their popularity in later years, and the accommodation was adapted and modernised. Consequently, it is not always easy to distinguish the medieval layout, although the character of the later works was usually influenced by the earlier buildings.

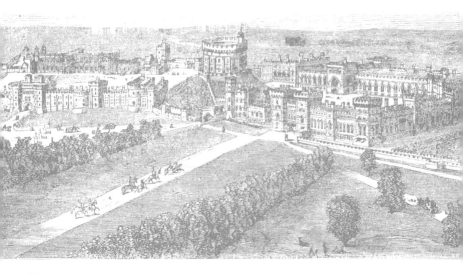

Buda Castle

Although there had been a royal castle at Buda, in Hungary, since the 13th century, the site was rebuilt on a palatial scale by King Sigismund I in the early 15th century. Coinciding with his election, in 1410, as Holy Roman Emperor in waiting, this was probably undertaken to provide Sigismund with a residence to befit his enhanced status. The castle has an elevated site above the River Danube, with the outer defences extending down to the river.

Wawel Royal Castle

Wawel, in Krakow, Poland, holds both the cathedral and the royal castle. The castle was rebuilt in the 14th century, but a fire in 1499 gave King Sigismund I the opportunity to remodel it further and create a magnificent Renaissance palace.

The Louvre

Built from 1190–1202 by Philip II Augustus, the Louvre, in Paris, was a quadrangular castle with cylindrical corner towers and donjon. In 1364, the master mason Raymond du Temple transformed it into a royal palace for Charles V. Key architectural features were a great spiral staircase housed in its own turret, and a gallery linking the new apartments of the north range to the refurbished donjon.

Baronial Stronghold

While the monarch was usually the greatest castle holder in the realm, the vast majority of castles were in the hands of the secular nobility. Some nobles possessed several castles, but apart from those of the greatest lords, which might have a wider territorial spread, they tended to be confined to the particular geographical region in which the lord was based. Just as royal castles were symbols of a king's authority, those of his subordinate aristocracy were reminders of their wealth and power within their own domains.

Château de Coucy
Enguerrand III, Lord of Coucy, in Picardy, France, reconstructed his ancestral home on an irregularly shaped plateau from c.1225. A powerful sense of his own importance, engendered no doubt by his martial prowess and family connections with the English and French royal houses, is reflected in the scale of the castle. It comprised not only the tightly packed inner ward shown here, but also a large outer ward and fortified town. The cylindrical great tower that overlooked the castle was the largest in Europe.

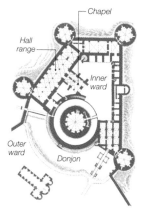

Chapel

Hall range

Inner ward

Outer ward

Donjon

The inner ward: Château de Coucy (plan)

Dominating the entrance is the massive donjon, its encircling chemise wall forming part of the curtain. There were also four angle towers. Access to the inner ward was via a gateway east of the donjon, approached by a fortified bridge and protected by a twin portcullis. A passage led to the courtyard and on to the main domestic accommodation.

The lord's residence: Château de Coucy

The inner ward, which contained the best apartments, was the lord's residence. Siting the lord's quarters in the remotest part of the castle was a commonly observed tenet of castle design. To the right is the chapel, to the left the gateway from the outer ward, and between them the donjon.

Kenilworth Castle

Founded c.1120, Kenilworth became a highly strategic fortress protected by a large artificial lake, and was held by some of the most powerful men in England: Simon de Montfort, Earl of Leicester in the 13th century, and John of Gaunt, Duke of Lancaster in the 14th century.

Burg Eltz

Sometimes castles came under joint ownership, requiring separate domestic accommodation for different branches of the family. Burg Eltz contained accommodation for six households, all clustered around the main courtyard and vying for space in the high-rise main block.

Fortified Manor House

The core of Aydon Castle, in Northumberland, was built as a manor house in the late 13th century. Almost immediately hostilities broke out between England and Scotland, and the border counties became a war zone. Fortification was carried out in several stages over the next 50 years to create a small enclosure castle based around three courtyards. While Aydon might now be considered a fortified manor house, it is notable that in 1415 it was listed as a castle.

Some lesser-defended residences are distinguished from castles by the appellation 'fortified manor house'. While this is a modern classification, it is clear that different degrees of fortification were sometimes recognised in the medieval period. This is evident in a document of 1415, which lists the castles and fortalices (defended manor houses) in Northumberland; it represents a serious attempt to distinguish one type of establishment from the other. Drawing the line is not always easy, as the compilers of the list discovered when some entries had to be corrected. For our purposes it is debatable as to how useful an exercise it might be. Fortification of residences is always a matter of degree, varying according to function.

38

Acton Burnell Castle

Acton Burnell Castle was built c.1284 by Robert Burnell, Bishop of Bath and Wells and Chancellor to Edward I, at his birthplace in Shropshire, close to the Welsh border. Although it was not a serious defensive work, it included a number of security measures. An original and compact design, the main accommodation was at first-floor level, there was a crenellated parapet, and the house was probably surrounded by a moat and possibly a fence.

Kitchen

Hall   Tower

Gateway

Yanwath Hall (with plan)

Yanwath, in Cumbria, is another border manor house dating from the late medieval period when cross-border raiding was endemic and residences needed to be secure. Here, the defensive element is centred on a tower attached to one end of the hall. It appears to have had two principal construction phases, in the 14th and 15th centuries. Now a courtyard house, only two of the three ranges bordering the quadrangle are medieval in date, although it may have been enclosed by a pale or wall.

Castellated House

Herstmonceux Castle
Herstmonceux, dating from c.1441, boasts towers, interval turrets, crenellations, a wide moat and a substantial gatehouse. This last had a drawbridge, portcullis, gun loops, arrow loops, a machicolated gallery and a recessed entrance protected by murder holes. However, the castle's regularity, its tactically weak position and the tranquil nature of the scene suggest that aesthetic pleasure was the main motive in its construction.

Some castles were always less military in character than others. Fortification came at a cost, and a man cut his coat according to his cloth and the perceived level of vulnerability to attack. In the later medieval period, however, the military trappings of castles – crenellations, portcullises, machicolations, and so forth – became fashionable because they were thought of as being appropriate to a lordly dwelling. Many later castles, therefore, may be thought of as castellated country houses rather than serious fortresses. Herstmonceux in Sussex, for example, is on the cusp of castle and country house: clues to its builder's true intent lie in its location (in a dip overlooked by surrounding hills), its character and its design.

Thornbury Castle
Begun in 1507, Thornbury Castle, in Gloucestershire, is a link between the medieval castle and the post-medieval country house. Externally, it had the appearance of a fortress, being provided with towers, gun loops, and a gatehouse with portcullis, but within the outer walls the emphasis was on a gracious domesticity.

Oxburgh Hall
Despite being built under a 1482 licence to crenellate, Oxburgh Hall, in Norfolk, is essentially domestic in character. It is moated, but there are no corner towers, and although the parapets are crenellated, they sit on pseudo-machicolations and are principally for show.

Bodiam Castle
The nature of Herstmonceux may have been inspired by the castle of Bodiam, also in Sussex, built half a century earlier. A tightly planned quadrangular castle surrounded by a wide moat, Bodiam set a standard for the castellated but picturesque centrepiece in a planned landscape.

Introduction

Bamburgh Castle

Bamburgh Castle, on the Northumberland coast, was fortified as early as the 6th century, and contains 12th-, 13th- and 14th-century phases. The site's topography restricted the design, resulting in an elongated plan that followed the contours of the underlying rock. With the early medieval castle established, there was little room for manoeuvre in the design of any subsequent additions.

In designing a castle it was rare to have the luxury of a site without topographical restrictions. These were either – in the case of virgin sites – because of the difficult terrain of a defendable location, or – in the case of established sites – because of the need to accommodate an existing layout or incorporate existing buildings. Some sites were already ancient by the time of the Norman conquest in 1066, and present a long history of modification, adaptation and renewal. In early castles defence tended to be a greater consideration than in the later Middle Ages, and the tactical advantages of a site were more highly prized. Later it was often the architectural character of the castle that was the priority.

Kitchen

Keep

Great hall

Inner bailey

Gateway

Living quarters

Kenilworth Castle (plan)

Probably of early 12th-century origin, Kenilworth Castle, in Warwickshire, may have begun life as a motte and bailey castle, and it is possible that the later 12th-century keep is on the site of the original motte. By the 14th century, when the castle came to Richard II's uncle (John of Gaunt, Duke of Lancaster), the castle covered a much greater area. The buildings of the original bailey were remodelled to create a group of palatial domestic apartments in which the lines of the 12th-century castle were, to a great extent, retained.

Calahorra Tower

There are numerous instances of building adaptation. One example of a structure whose function changed during the Middle Ages is the Calahorra Tower in Cordoba, Spain. Originally a twin-towered gatehouse of the Islamic period, it was converted into a tower in the 14th century. The gateway was blocked by being infilled at the front, and having a square turret built to the rear. In addition, flanking quarter-circle links were built in the angle between the old gatehouse and the new turret.

Castello d'Estense

Occasionally a castle builder had the advantage of an unhindered site and could give free reign to his aesthetic sense. Castello d'Estense in Ferrara, northern Italy, by architect Bartolino da Novara, is a fine example of this. A quadrangular castle built on a flat site, the regularity of the structure gives it the look of a great house rather than a military building, despite it being fortified with a moat, defended gateways and machicolations.

Architectural Effect

Steinsberg Castle
Built in the early
12th century and
rebuilt during the
13th, Steinsberg Castle
occupies a hilltop in
Baden-Würtemberg,
Germany. It is built to
a comparatively simple
design, with concentric
fortifications around an
inner courtyard housing
an octagonal great
tower. Regardless of the
defensive considerations
that lay behind its siting
and layout, the castle
makes a striking visual
impact. The combination
of octagonal tower and
faceted inner courtyard
wall is a deliberate
attempt to create an
effective massing of
reflective shapes.

There is no doubt that, from an early date, castle builders were considering the outward effect of their compositions. One aspect of this was a desire to create displays of power and to instil awe – a useful tool in intimidating an enemy or recalcitrant populace. However, it is evident that aesthetics were also a consideration, particularly from the 12th century onwards. Castles were not only fortifications, but also status symbols whereby the builder could advertise his wealth, importance and taste. An elevated position served to enhance the architectural effect.

Baronial tower

There was a timber castle at Stafford by the early 12th century. In 1348 Ralph, First Earl of Stafford, built a great tower on top of the old motte, perhaps to promote his newly acquired wealth and status. It was an imposing building with octagonal turrets at the angles and a semi-octagonal turret in the centre of the south front. This faced the main road between Stafford and the Welsh Marches, and the building seems to have been sited to achieve the maximum architectural effect.

Warkworth Castle

The donjon of Warkworth Castle, built for Henry Percy, First Earl of Northumberland, in the late 14th century, represents a high point in great tower design. This residence was built to an unusual plan to contain a compact and ingeniously arranged interior. Positioning the donjon on top of the Norman motte takes full advantage of the dramatic possibilities of the site. The heraldic device of the Percy family is displayed on the front of the north turret – an emphatic proclamation of ownership.

Manzanares el Real

In the later Middle Ages there was a tendency for the martial appearance of a castle to become an end in itself. The defensive aspects of a design might be functional, but they were also desirable. In the 15th century fashion sometimes overrode function so that military forms evolved into purely decorative motifs. At Manzanares el Real, near Madrid, the gallery's machicolations are false, serving solely to contribute to an ornamental effect.

Symbolism

Caernarfon Castle
Caernarfon Castle, in Gwynedd, was intended to evoke Constantinople, capital of the Eastern Roman Empire. The princes of Gwynedd traced their ancestry to Magnus Maximus, who established himself as Roman Emperor in 383 BCE. Tradition associated Maximus with the Roman town of Segontium, close to Caernarfon. With this castle, Edward was portraying himself as the successor of the Emperor and his supposed descendants, the Welsh princes.

Expressions of power and authority were part and parcel of the architectural character of castles, their martial features reflecting the military nature of the medieval aristocracy and identifying the owner as a member of the nobility. In a few cases castle builders were more subtle and specific in their intent, which may have been to give expression and/or support to a political concept. Only occasionally is it possible to interpret the intent of the builder in such cases, and only by careful research into the historical context of the building can apparent idiosyncrasies in the design be associated with a doctrinal message. One of the most convincing interpretations of symbolism concerns Caernarfon Castle in North Wales, begun by Edward I in 1283, following his annexation of Gwynedd, at the heart of the old Welsh principality.

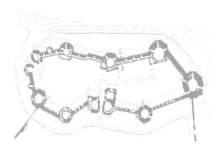

Caernarfon Castle (plan)

The plan of Caernarfon Castle was partly determined by the earthworks of the 11th-century Norman castle on which it was built. This lent it an added symbolism by inferring that Edward, King of England, was legitimately reclaiming lands that had been captured by the Welsh.

Ashby-de-la-Zouche Castle

Additions or refurbishments might proclaim a recently acquired status. William Lord Hastings' conversion of Ashby–de-la-Zouche manor house into a castle was linked to his status as one of Edward IV's most influential servants. The great tower that rises above the hall is a potent symbol of lordship.

Dunstanburgh Castle

Built c.1313 for King Edward II's cousin and rival, Thomas Earl of Lancaster, the design of Dunstanburgh promoted the Earl's perception of himself. Lancaster, who identified with the mythical King Arthur, enhanced the isolation of the coastal headland site by constructing man-made water features to evoke the island of Avalon.

Façade: Dunstanburgh Castle

The principal feature of Dunstanburgh is its gatehouse, which draws inspiration from the royal castle of Harlech, dating from the 1280s. To some extent, however, it is a façade, the upper parts being little more than a screen. Its main purpose may have been purely to be highly visible from the sea.

Castle Builders

Master James of St George

Master mason James of St George is an example of the geographical reach a castle builder could have, given the right connections. Not only did he work on the Count of Savoy's castles in Switzerland, but he also masterminded Edward I's great castle-building programme in Wales, of which Conwy (below) was part.

The castle builder had to reconcile the needs of a great house with those of a fortress. In consequence, the role ranged from that of military engineer to domestic architect, the patron specifying requirements and the master builder encompassing them within the confines of the available site. Many early military engineers had a background in carpentry and were also concerned with the construction of siege engines, but where stone was the principal building material, it was the mason who called the tune. Competent master masons were much valued, some having international reputations.

Clifford's Tower: section view

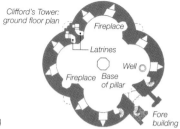

Clifford's Tower: ground floor plan

Fireplace

Latrines

Well

Fireplace

Base of pillar

Fore building

Henry de Reyns (section and plan)
Crowning the top of the Norman motte of York Castle, Clifford's Tower was built between 1245 and 1260 to a quatrefoil plan. Henry III's master mason, Henry de Reyns, is credited with the design.

Henry de Reyns also masterminded the reconstruction of Westminster Abbey, which reflected recent architectural developments in France. The plan of Clifford's Tower, too, has a French parallel in the 12th-century great tower at Étampes near Paris.

Francesco di Giorgio Martini
By virtue of his book, *Trattato di Architettura Civile e Militare*, Francesco di Giorgio Martini is one of the few castle builders who can be studied through their drawings and writings. Rocca di Cagli, built in central Italy in 1481, was one of the many fortresses built by Francesco for his patron, the Duke of Urbino.

John Lewyn
John Lewyn was one of the most prolific English castle builders of the later 14th century: he worked widely across the northern region. The unconventional outer gatehouse of Carlisle Castle (above), which was built by Lewyn from 1378, adheres to the compact and intricately planned designs with which he is most associated.

49

Use of Geometry

While castle planning was, to a great extent, determined by defensive considerations and the topographical nature of the site, geometry played a major role from the 11th century onwards, firstly in the design of individual elements, and ultimately as the basis for entire castles. Symmetrical castles were being built from the 13th century and, as the architectural character of the castle rivalled or took precedence over its defensive aspects in the 14th century, the natural approach for a new site was a geometrically inspired plan.

Symmetrical defence
In this drawing from Francesco di Giorgio Martini's architectural treatise, the geometrical foundation of the design is plainly evident. A square great tower stands in the centre of a square enclosure with circular corner towers. The interior of the enclosure is divided by walls, arranged in the form of a St Andrew's cross, that extend from the corners of the great tower to the angle towers.

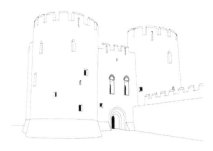

Great tower: Dudley Castle

Dudley Castle, in the West Midlands, crowns a prominent hilltop. The great tower, which occupies the Norman motte, was begun in the 1260s. The simple, but effective composition, in which a central block is massed together with corner turrets, has a pure geometrical basis, and was influenced by contemporary gatehouse design.

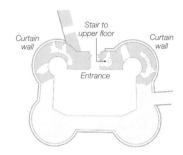

Great tower: Dudley Castle (plan)

Dudley's great tower was not necessarily planned as an integrated part of a wider complex. It could have been designed independently. The impression is of a building designed primarily for effect. The accommodation was simple; more comfortable quarters were probably to be found in the bailey.

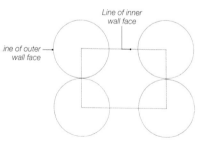

The geometrical basis (plan)

The ground plan for Dudley Castle was a rectangle with four circles centred on the corners. The common diameter of the circles equalled the length of the short side of the rectangle. This gives the internal line of the main block and the external line of the turrets. All that remained was to decide on the wall thicknesses and openings.

A proportional system (plan)

Many medieval buildings were built to a proportional system of measurement. The plan of the late-14th-century castle of Lumley, in County Durham, is based on the equation 1:$\sqrt{2}$, or the relationship of the side of a square (1) to its diagonal ($\sqrt{2}$). It can be found in the general layout, towers and rooms.

Timber

The timber tower
Although no timber castle towers survive, both pictorial and archaeological evidence confirm their former existence. The bas-relief below depicts two timber towers and gives clues to their structural character. Both have inclined corner timbers joined by horizontal beams and St Andrew's cross bracing, and both are crenellated.

While stone is now the building material most associated with castles, the majority of early castles were timber, and timber remained a major component in castle construction throughout the medieval period. The perishable nature of the material, and the comparative ease with which it can be dismantled for reuse, mean that most timber structures have perished, so we are left with a distorted view of its former significance. However, although there are now few traces of medieval castle timberwork, there is ample evidence for its former existence.

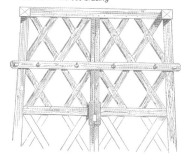
St Andrew's cross bracing

Medieval bell towers

While timber castle towers have disappeared, something of their structural character can be deduced from surviving medieval bell towers. Some of these display carpentry traits that tally with those shown in medieval illustrations such as this, including the tapering sides and the St Andrew's cross bracing. They provide models for the reconstruction of their timber counterparts.

A timber enceinte

Castles were usually a mixture of timber and stone elements, as is clearly illustrated by this medieval manuscript drawing in which the stone buildings within the enceinte are enclosed by a timber palisade. The depiction of this surrounding wall gives the impression of a well-carpentered structure provided with arrow loops and hinged shutters to the crenels. The timber gatehouse also has arrow loops and an oversailing crenellated parapet supported on bracing.

Windsor Castle

Owing to the widespread destruction of castles, most medieval timberwork is no longer extant. However, in buildings that have been continuously occupied since the Middle Ages, some examples do survive. One of these buildings is the royal castle of Windsor. This illustration shows a detail from the Canons' Cloister of c.1353, adjacent to St George's Chapel.

Masonry Types

Ashlar with rubble infill
In the Middle Ages the best-quality masonry was ashlar, which consisted of squared and finely dressed stone blocks. Ashlar, which came into widespread usage for wall faces around 1100, demanded a high level of skill and a lengthy preparation. Stones were cut to shape and size in the masons' lodge, then transported to site to be placed in position. The good-quality stone required could sometimes be procured only from a source a considerable distance from the site.

A standard method of walling in the medieval period was to build two stone faces and to infill the space between them with a mixture of rubble and mortar. While this structural concept was universal, castles exhibit a wide variety of masonry styles. Certain practices have a degree of chronological significance, but other influential factors were the accessibility of materials, regional custom, and the funding available.

Coursed rubble

A cheaper alternative to ashlar was rubble. Rubble was usually local stone readily available from quarries opened close to the site to keep transport costs low. The level of technical training required was not so great, and preparation of the stone was carried out on site as and when required during the course of construction.

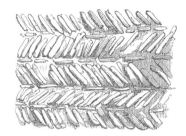

Herringbone masonry

Herringbone masonry, a distinctive type of coursed stonework favoured in the 11th century, is thought to have been a method used when speed was required. The courses were set obliquely, with the direction of the pitch alternating between them. These oblique courses were sometimes separated by horizontal levelling courses.

Rusticated masonry

In rusticated or 'bossed' masonry, fashionable in the 12th-century Crusader states, the margins of the stone blocks were cleanly trimmed while the raised centres were more coarsely treated. At Beaufort Castle, Lebanon, the rustication is graded so that the door and window surrounds are more finely finished than the ordinary walls.

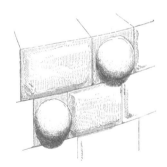

Isabelline masonry

Bossed masonry of a different kind was popular in Spain during the Isabelline period of the late 15th century, notably at the castle of Manzanares el Real near Madrid. These round bosses, which have been likened to cannonballs, are purely ornamental features that contribute to a highly florid decorative scheme.

Masonry Details

Medieval wall facings give a good indication of the nature of stone construction. However, they are not the only aspects of masonry work to serve as clues to the process of castle building. Some facets of stone wall construction, such as mortar consistency and structural ironwork, are not as visible or accessible as others, yet still provide data about the construction of a building. Masons' marks supply evidence for the building process and its organisation, and reused stonework, where it can be recognised for what it is, gives clues regarding the supply of materials.

Recycled stone
Many castles are on or close to ancient sites. The practice of reusing old masonry was widely followed by medieval builders as it saved time, effort and cost. Recycled stonework was often used as rubble, either for facings or for the core. Occasionally, however, the quality was good enough for masonry to be used without reworking, as at the Crusader castle of Gibelet, in Lebanon, where the ruins of ancient Byblos were extensively reused.

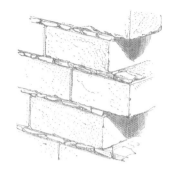

Wide mortar joints

In rubble constructions, or those built with roughly squared stones as opposed to ashlar blocks, the tendency was to lay mortar courses thickly in order to even out the irregularities of the stonework. Such widely spaced courses are sometimes an indication of early masonry work.

Aggregate in mortar

In some cases, the levelling function of thick mortar layers was assisted by the inclusion of aggregate in the form of small hard stones or tiles. Such inclusions also increased the compressive strength of the mortar courses, which helped to maintain the structural integrity of a building.

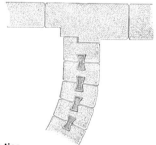

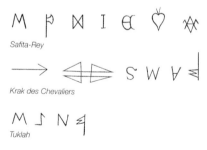

Safita-Rey

Krak des Chevaliers

Tuklah

Iron ties

To strengthen ashlar construction, iron ties were sometimes incorporated to create a 'chain' of masonry. At Sidon, in Lebanon, ties were used to strengthen a semi-circular building. The ties are set within insets cut into the bedding planes of the masonry, to provide resistance to lateral thrust.

Masons' marks

Ashlar blocks sometimes bear masons' marks – the unique identification marks of the masons who cut the blocks. They were probably used for quality control, or in calculating piecework payments. Masons cut the stones to shape in a temporary building known as a lodge.

Vaults & Floors

Castles, or elements within them, were frequently multi-storey buildings, so the structural issues of flooring and vaulting were important considerations for the medieval castle builder. A number of different masonry construction methods were in use. In those parts of the castle with a military function, strength was important, but the choice of technique might also be determined by cost, regional practice and the availability of materials, or by suitability to serve a particular design function.

Tunnel vaulting

Tunnel vaulting was often used to cover lower-storey rooms, though it is less common at higher levels. In the 14th-century tower house of Dacre Castle, in Cumbria, the main basement rooms have plain tunnel vaults while the entrance passage vaults are augmented with transverse ribs. Stone vaulting provided both fireproofing and a solid base on which to construct the upper floors.

Rib vaulting

While tunnel vaulting provided solidity, rib vaulting produced a better aesthetic effect. Consequently, it was occasionally used to produce a sense of grandeur. In the great hall of Margat Castle, in Syria, the structural nature of the feature is exposed. The ribs, which spring from corbels, provide a framework to support the intervening panels of stone webbing. The surfaces above are levelled with mortar and rubble infill, which sets to a solid mass.

Corbels

Where the lower storey wasn't vaulted, a common method of floor construction was to provide a series of sockets and corresponding corbels in the side walls to support the ends of the transverse beams, as in this 15th-century example at Castle Campbell, in Scotland. Where the timber floors have disappeared, the remaining corbels bear witness to the construction method.

Offsets

An alternative to corbelling was the offset, in which the inner face of the upper storey wall was set back from that of the lower storey to create a ledge on which the timberwork of the floor was then supported. This method was used in Conisborough's later 12-century cylindrical keep. This simple system resulted in a storey-by-storey narrowing of the walls.

Tower Construction

The tower was a specialist form of castle building. It had to withstand both the impact of missiles and the effects of mining, so soundness of construction was paramount. The technical advances of 12th-century architecture enabled the introduction of the cylindrical form. The rounded surface added deflective qualities and the circular plan offered a greater resistance to mining due to the absence of corners. Structural stability could be enhanced through the use of vaulting. Château de Coucy, in Picardy, France, had several outstanding examples of the tower builder's craft.

Wall tower

Coucy's wall tower is circular externally, but hexagonal internally. Each face contains an arched embrasure or recess framing a loop. The pattern alternates from floor to floor so that the feet of the upper recesses stand on the apexes of the lower tier. This allows the loops to be staggered, which provides a greater field of fire and gives structural strength with economy of materials.

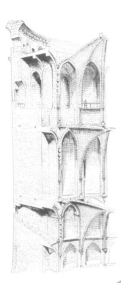

Donjon

The strength and stability of the cylindrical great tower relied on technological virtuosity rather than solidity of construction. The internal wall surfaces were covered with arched recesses, the piers between them acting as buttressing for a series of ribbed vaults over the central space that bound the structure together.

Vaulting detail

This detail of the donjon's second-floor gallery vaulting shows one of the main recess arches to the right, the face of an intervening pier in the centre, and the arched opening of one of the mural passages that connect the recesses. The recess is covered with a ribbed transverse tunnel vault; the connecting passage is roofed separately at a slightly lower level with a plain lateral tunnel vault. The intersection of different vaults and wall planes is testimony to a high degree of forward planning and precision workmanship.

Recess and passage vaulting (plan)

The interior of the cylindrical tower is dodecagonal (12-sided). The 12 ribs of the main vault (A) spring from imposts set between the splayed recesses. The recesses (D) are covered by individual tunnel vaults carried on two ribs (B and C). The sections are linked by short passages, which are vaulted separately at a lower level.

Scaffolding

Medieval construction was aided by the use of timber scaffolding raised in concert with the walls of a building. Some scaffolding was freestanding, but in many cases it was partially or entirely supported by the walls of the building. In these cases, horizontal timbers, or putlogs, were inserted into putlog holes. These were square apertures specially prepared by the masons within the stone coursing. Although the scaffolding itself is no longer in evidence, its character can sometimes be discerned through the surviving putlog holes.

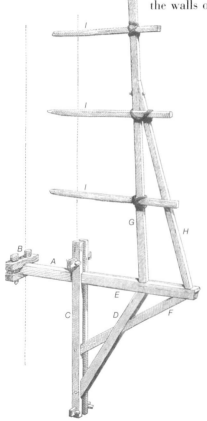

Reconstruction of scaffold

Scaffolding systems could vary considerably and depended on the nature of the building and the regional practices of the carpenters. Reference to medieval illustrations and surviving examples of contemporary woodwork help us to understand the character of such temporary structures. In this example, the main horizontal beam (A) extends right through the wall and is anchored on the internal face with a clamp secured by wedges (B). It is further clamped on the outside by vertical timbers (C), which also act as a support for the bracing (D, E, F). Above the main beam a post (G), stiffened by a brace (H), carries a series of beams (I) that are keyed into the wall face. These beams carry the platforms.

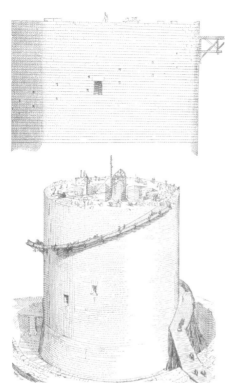

Putlog holes

Putlog holes usually appear regularly spaced in horizontal lines. At Château de Coucy in Picardy, France, however, the paired (one above another) putlog holes around the cylindrical donjon (c.1220) are in a spiral pattern, suggesting that the medieval scaffold was inclined. This is an arrangement that was also used in 13th-century Savoy, whence it was imported to North Wales by the Savoyard craftsmen employed by Edward I during his vast castle-building programme there during the last quarter of the century.

Reconstruction of spiral scaffold

A reconstruction of the spiral scaffold around the donjon shows how this system probably worked. The platform served as a gently inclined plane that could be used to transport materials and equipment to the top of the walls, which formed the working surface.

Reconstruction of timberwork

This reconstruction suggests the timberwork used for raising the Coucy donjon. Horizontal beams (A and B) extend into and beyond the wall face. They are clasped by paired posts at the point of entry (C) and towards the end of the lower beam (D). A series of diagonal braces (E, F, G, H) provides rigidity.

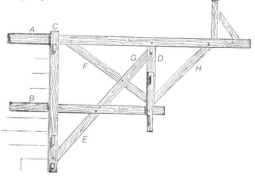

Embellishment

Gate arch

Gate arch
The main route to the
lord's apartments was
often picked out for
emphasis. Both ends
of the 12th-century
entrance into the shell
keep at Alnwick Castle,
in Northumberland, were
given a richly sculptured
gate arch, impressive
enough to be retained
during the 14th-century
remodelling.

Castles are sometimes thought of as functional
buildings with minimal decoration. However, the
often ruinous remains we see today probably give a
false impression. There are examples of sculptural
embellishment, for instance, surviving from the 11th
century onwards, and these, together with other known
aspects of medieval ornamental work, make it clear
that decoration was often a consideration of the castle
builder from the outset. The remains of any
embellishment indicate to which parts of the castle the
builder wished attention to be drawn.

The carved capital

In aisled halls, as in aisled churches, the capitals of the arcade columns were objects of the sculptor's art. These crocket capitals (carved to resemble leaves), c.1200, in the great hall of Oakham Castle in Rutland, might indeed be mistaken for ecclesiastical work. They are typical of the unusually rich sculptural decoration at Oakham, where no expense was spared in the embellishment of the stonework.

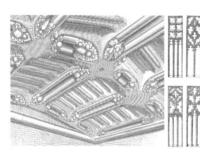

The decorative ceiling

In this 14th-century ceiling, now in Naworth Castle, in Cumbria, all elements are heavily moulded and embellished by the stylised undulating foliage characteristic of the period. The panels between the joists (shown on the right) are carved with blind tracery. Bosses decorated some intersections. Some of this work would also have been painted.

The monumental fireplace

The great hall, the most public of domestic rooms, served as a ceremonial chamber in which the owner's wealth might be displayed. This double fireplace, from Château de Coucy's late-14th-century great hall, was at once functional and a superb architectural focal point, being surmounted by nine greater than life-size statues.

Introduction

Beeston Castle

Built in the 1220s by Ranulph de Blundeville, Earl of Chester, Beeston Castle is sited on an impressive bluff that dominates the adjacent plain. Protected on two sides by a cliff, and elsewhere by steeply sloping sides, it presents a tactically advantageous site for a fortress, and was indeed developed as such in the prehistoric period. Ranulph's outer defences overlie the prehistoric defences, which were probably visible when he came to build his castle.

Castles are often classified according to a number of broad physical types. There is sometimes a degree of overlap, but it is usually possible to discern the prevalence of one type, and the initial identification is a useful starting point for interpretation. One type that could be classified in more than one way is the castle that makes use of an existing fortified site. The adaptation of existing fortifications and other occupied sites was indeed a widespread phenomenon among castle builders, particularly in the early period. They provided obvious defensive positions that could be brought into a state of readiness relatively quickly. In warfare, this was a distinct advantage. However, it is also true that older fortifications were often situated in centres of population that might need to be protected or controlled.

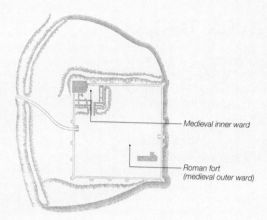

Portchester Castle (plan)

The builders of the coastal castle of Portchester, in Hampshire, made use of the defences of a Roman fort. The Anglo-Saxons had already reused the fort as a defended settlement, which makes the choice of site even more explicable. At Portchester the 11th-century castle was built in one corner of the fort, making use of the existing walls, and was separated from the greater enclosure by a ditch.

Medieval inner ward

Roman fort (medieval outer ward)

Old Sarum Castle

Old Sarum, north of the later city of Salisbury, in Wiltshire, was built within an Iron Age hillfort. The site contained an Anglo-Saxon town or *burh* and was therefore a centre of population and commerce that had to be controlled. The Normans built an enclosure castle, demarcated by a bank and outer ditch, within the centre of the site. This castle is 0.7 ha (1¾ acres) in area compared with the 11.9 ha (29½ acres) of the greater enclosure.

Castel Sant'Angelo

Castel Sant'Angelo, in Rome, results from the fortification of Hadrian's mausoleum of c.135 CE in the early medieval period. The mausoleum, which comprised a giant rotunda set on a square podium, and which determined the plan of the later castle, is now enclosed within a square curtain wall with 15th-century polygonal towers projecting from the angles.

Motte & Bailey

In this hypothetical motte and bailey castle, the bailey, to the left, is surrounded by a timber palisade. Entry is via a bridge and gate at the furthest point from the motte. The entrance to the motte is from the bailey only, via a gate and then a bridge across the intervening ditch. This approach receives further protection from palisades that extend up the slope of the motte. The motte itself is crowned by another gated palisade and by a tower.

An early type of castle that proliferated during the Norman conquest of England was the motte and bailey, in which a ditched earthen mound (the motte) was combined with a ditched enclosure (the bailey). The motte provided an elevated site for a lookout post, often enhanced by a tower, and a tactically advantageous position from which to conduct the defence of the castle. The bailey protected the domestic accommodation, stores and other necessaries. The structures of motte and bailey castles were of timber to begin with, but in many cases these were later replaced with stone.

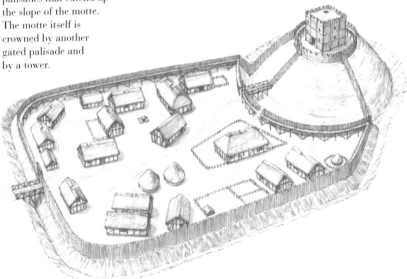

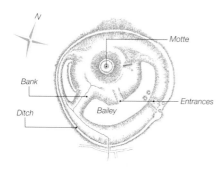

Builth Castle (plan)

Builth in Powys, Wales, was founded towards the end of the 11th century and completely rebuilt in stone in the 1270s. Even so, the earthworks are all that remain. A circular motte and sub-circular bank and ditch define a kidney-shaped bailey. Initial access was across the outer ditch to the bailey, and from the bailey to the motte.

Berkhamsted Castle (plan)

Berkhamsted Castle was in existence by 1086. An oval bailey and detached motte are surrounded by a water-filled ditch or moat, contained by a bank. This, in turn, is surrounded by a second moat, beyond which is another bank incorporating projecting platforms or bastions. How much of this dates from the 11th century is unclear.

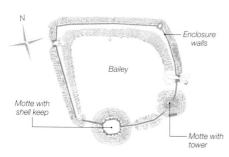

Lincoln Castle (plan)

Lincoln Castle, which dates from 1068, is unusual in having two mottes. The larger motte is surmounted by the 12th-century shell keep; the smaller supports a square tower of Norman origin. However, the relative dates of the mounds are uncertain.

Reconstruction: La Tusque

The motte and bailey site of La Tusque in Sainte-Eulalie d'Ambarès, south-west France, is unusual in having a rectangular bailey with a centrally sited motte. Three sides of the bailey were bordered by streams and the fourth by a ditch.

Great Tower & Courtyard

Château de Kaysersberg
Kaysersberg, in Alsace, France, was built for the Holy Roman Emperor Frederick II in the 1220s. It is set on a hillside above the town and the River Weiss. It has a triangular courtyard and, at its highest point, a cylindrical great tower, which adds to the commanding presence of the fortress.

The two great components of the stone castle were the great tower (or keep) and the courtyard, both of which might be considered as distinct forms of defensive architecture, although the combination of the two elements was common. Because of this widespread association with courtyard defences, great towers have often been considered as places of last resort, or as the final tier of a sequence of defences. While there may be some truth in this theory, its significance has undoubtedly been exaggerated in the past, and the interaction of great tower and courtyard are better understood on an individual basis. Keeps may sometimes have been seen as prestige buildings in their own right, and may even have been designed in relative isolation, rather than as an integral part of the castle. The great tower of Conisbrough Castle, in South Yorkshire, is an example of this.

Conisbrough Castle (plan)

Conisbrough keep stands close to one corner of the bailey rather than being freestanding within it, and has one segment forming part of the enceinte. Keeps have sometimes been considered as buildings designed for a passive defence or a place of last resort. This cannot be true of Conisbrough, where the keep is placed aggressively and was capable of playing a part in the defence of the curtain.

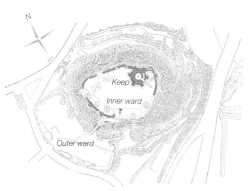

Masonry: Conisbrough Castle

The ashlar construction of Conisbrough keep contrasts markedly with the rubble walling of the adjacent curtain that abuts it on both sides. It is clear that the keep was thought of as a separate entity, and that integration with the rest of the castle was not a prime consideration of the architect from the outset.

Portillo Castle

The 15th-century Spanish castle of Portillo is a quadrangular complex with two concentric tiers of fortifications. The outer circuit is studded with rounded wall towers. At one corner of the enclosure, and dominating this part of the castle, is the rectangular great tower. It is arguable whether the tower adds anything to the military conception of the design: its presence may owe as much to tradition and architectural preference as to necessity.

Enclosure Castles

Ringworks

An early kind of enclosure castle, which predates the motte and bailey, is the ringwork. This type was in use at the time of the Norman conquest of England. Most ringwork castles were built of timber, and those that weren't redeveloped in stone survive only as earthworks. In these a bank and ditch define a roughly circular bailey. Like motte and bailey castles, ringworks sometimes have more than one bailey.

Despite being a recurrent feature in castle architecture, the great tower, or keep, was not always deemed necessary, and it is arguable as to how useful it was in military terms. Enclosure castles are encountered from the early medieval period onwards. Although the motte and bailey is sometimes considered the universal type during the Norman conquest of England, a sizeable proportion of early Norman castles were, in fact, enclosure castles. Late 12th- and 13th-century developments in military architecture were focused on the enceinte rather than the keep, and in many later medieval castles the great tower was eschewed in favour of a symmetrical arrangement of lodgings around a courtyard.

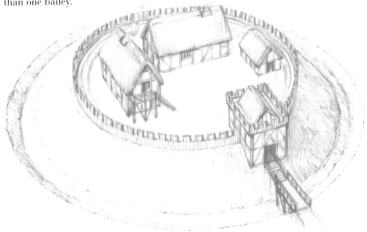

King John's Castle

King John's Castle, in Limerick, Ireland, was begun c.1210, by King John of England. It is sited by the River Shannon, and guarded the approach to the city from Thomond – a bridge across the river. In plan the castle was an irregular square with cylindrical corner towers. A gateway on the north side towards the road was flanked by twin D-shaped towers.

Kidwelly Castle (plan)

Founded in the early 12th century, Kidwelly, in South Wales, was a castle of enclosure from the outset. The half-moon-shaped outer enceinte represents the extent of the original timber castle's outline. In the late 13th century a quadrangular inner ward was built to contain the main domestic apartments.

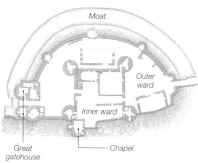

Moat

Outer ward

Inner ward

Great gatehouse

Chapel

Château de Grandson

Built on the north-west bank of Lake Neuchâtel in Switzerland, Château de Grandson dates principally from the 13th century, when it lay within the county of Savoy. During that period, Savoy had a special relationship with England, and there are stylistic links between castles of the two regions. Château de Grandson was the ancestral home of Otto de Grandson, who spent many years in the service of Edward I in England, Wales, France and the Holy Land. The castle forms an irregular rectangle with a number of irregularly spaced cylindrical towers.

Multiple Courtyards

Nottingham Castle
Founded by William the Conqueror in 1068, Nottingham Castle had something of a motte and bailey form, the 'motte' being a natural rock big enough to form the innermost of three baileys, the middle and outer baileys occupying progressively lower levels, and containing progressively less opulent accommodation. The approach was through the outer bailey to the middle bailey, and thence to the inner bailey.

Many castles had two baileys, and sometimes more, dividing the complex into several protected areas, each devoted to a different function. In such cases there was often a progression from one bailey to another. This plan denoted a hierarchical structure, with the lord's accommodation being based in the most remote part of the castle and lesser buildings being housed in the more accessible parts. Such sequences might also be woven into the pattern of defence. However, not all multiple-courtyard sites were laid out in such a manner, and in some there may have been a degree of independence between baileys.

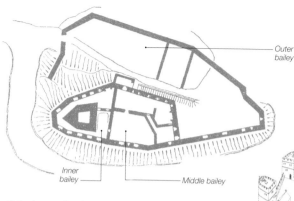

Outer bailey

Inner bailey

Middle bailey

Ortenbourg Castle (plan)

A three-bailey sequence, adapted to create
a powerful defensive arrangement, appears
at the 13th-century Ortenbourg Castle in
Alsace, France. The inner bailey occupies
the highest point, with the middle bailey at
a lower level immediately to the south, and
the outer bailey wrapped around the east
and south sides of this inner line of defence.
The approach from the outer gate to the
inner bailey is steep, circuitous and highly
controlled.

Alnwick Castle (right)

Alnwick Castle was first built in 1096, as a
motte with two baileys. The motte was later
partly levelled and a shell keep constructed
on its site at the junction of the two baileys.
In the 14th century this keep was lined
with apartments to enclose a third
courtyard. Since then, access has been
through the outer gate into the west bailey,
through the middle gate to the south of the
shell keep and into the east bailey, then
through the inner gate into the keep.

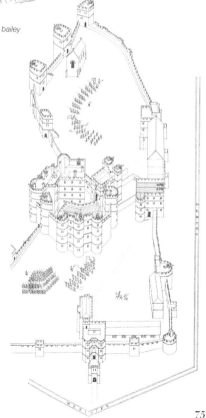

Concentric Castles

In the 1180s King Henry II raised a massive rectangular keep at Dover Castle, in Kent. He enclosed it within a curtain wall incorporating rectangular wall towers to create an inner ward. This itself was enclosed within the outer curtain. Although this was not fully concentric – the outer curtain only follows the line of the inner curtain on three sides – the arrangement shows that the general principle had been established.

The concentric castle is a type of multiple-courtyard castle that developed during the 13th century. This concept probably has its origins in the Middle East. Instead of a linear progression of baileys, the inner ward is surrounded by an outer ward of similar plan. In England and Wales it is particularly associated with King Edward I from the 1270s onwards, initially at the Tower of London, which received a line of outer defences at this time, and also during the conquest of Wales later in the century. Although castle building in Britain reached its culmination in the late 13th century, the idea of concentric fortification had been grasped during the reconstruction of Dover Castle nearly 100 years previously.

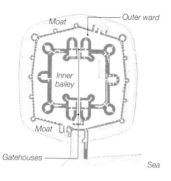

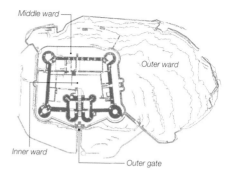

Beaumaris Castle (plan)

One of Edward I's Welsh castles, Beaumaris was begun in 1295 in order to control the Menai Straits and secure the sea route on which the Edwardian castles depended. The plan shows a confident symmetrical design made possible by a flat and unimpeded coastal site. The walls of the inner ward tower above those of the outer ward, and particular emphasis is placed on the two pairs of gatehouses.

Harlech Castle (plan)

Harlech is another of the chain of castles raised by Edward I of England during his conquest of Wales. Begun in 1283, after the conclusion of the Second Welsh War and the annexation of Gwynedd, it has a regular concentric plan. Although there is no great tower as such, that function was effectively fulfilled by the massive inner gatehouse, which contained the accommodation for the constable of the castle.

Wards: Harlech Castle

The outer ward of Harlech Castle, which is enclosed by a low curtain wall and entered via a small gatehouse, is largely military. The walls of the inner ward rise much higher. They overlook the outer ward, thus increasing the degree and angle of firepower that could be directed outside the castle at any one time, and rendering the outer ward untenable to an enemy should it be infiltrated.

Integrated Plan

Bolton Castle

Built c.1377–95 by master mason John Lewyn for Richard le Scrope, Bolton was erected in two or three principal phases. It is a large and complex design: five-storey rectangular corner towers, linked by two- and three-storey domestic ranges, enclose a quadrangular courtyard.

In early enclosure castles, the residential and defensive aspects were usually quite separate entities, architecturally as well as functionally. From the 13th century there was a tendency to integrate the domestic accommodation with the defences, to create a compact and often symmetrical plan. One of the earliest castles of this type is Castel del Monte, c.1240, in Puglia, Italy, but it was only in the 14th century, when numerous examples were built from new, that the integrated courtyard castle became a common type. One of the most ambitious examples in England is the late-14th-century Bolton Castle in North Yorkshire, which influenced several later buildings in northern England.

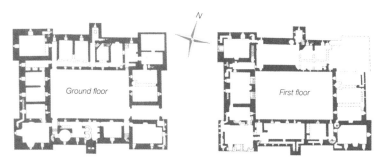

Ground-floor: Bolton Castle (plan)

The main gateway led into the courtyard from where five entrances gave access to the interior. In a large and complex house like Bolton, multiple entrances were a convenience, but also helped to control access. A large proportion of the ground floor was given over to services, including brewhouse, bakehouse, buttery and stables.

First-floor: Bolton Castle (plan)

The principal domestic apartments were focused on the first-floor great hall, at the west end of the north range. The great hall served as a public entrance to the residential suites in the west range and the western towers at first-floor level and above. Lesser lodgings were in the east and south ranges, with staff probably concentrated in the south-east quadrant.

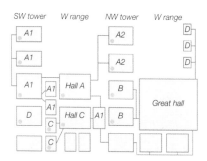

Planning diagram: Bolton Castle

An analysis of Bolton's interior reveals a sophisticated scheme of spatial planning with strict lines of communication. This extract shows a complex of residential suites (A, B and C) each of which is centred on a hall as well as a number of single-chamber lodgings (D).

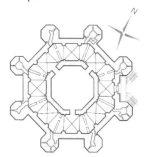

Castel del Monte (plan)

The forebear of most integrated castles is Castel del Monte, a hunting lodge of c.1240 built for the Holy Roman Emperor Frederick II on a hilltop in Puglia, Italy. Its symmetrical plan – a regular octagon – embodies a rarely achieved architectural and mathematical ideal.

Irregular Plan

Most castles were built to an irregular plan, a phenomenon that can usually be explained in topographical terms, owing to the fact that it was often the defensive capabilities of a site that were the principal reason for choosing to build a castle in a particular location. Hilltops, promontories and waterside locations were among the types of site that castle builders turned to advantage. This topographical basis meant that once the essentials of the layout had been established, they were unlikely to be radically altered, and later works were considerably constrained by the original plan.

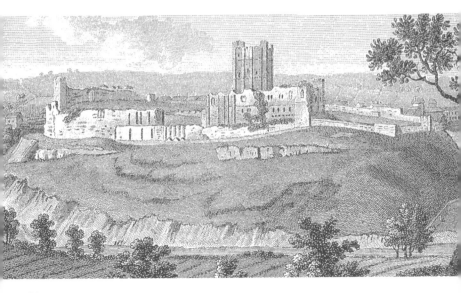

Peñafiel Castle

The elongated character of Peñafiel Castle, in northern Spain, is owed to its siting on a narrow ridge. It has the essential qualities of a Spanish type known as a *gran buque* (great ship). The inner curtain bristles with round towers and turrets and surrounds a slender enclosure. Rising high above the curtain, a three-storey square keep represents the bridge of the ship and acts as the architectural focus.

Krivoklát Castle

Another hilltop site is Krivoklát, in the Czech Republic, a castle of the kings of Bohemia. Initially constructed of timber, the site was rebuilt in stone during the late 13th century under Premsyl Otakar II and Václav II, and again between 1492–1522 under Vladislaus II. Krivoklát is built to an irregular triangular plan, with apartments ranged around two inner courtyards and a great cylindrical tower at the apex.

Haut-Koenigsbourg Castle (plan)

The 12th-century castle at Haut-Koenigsbourg was largely rebuilt in the late 15th century, and again at the end of the 19th century. The peculiar plan is owed to the nature of the mountaintop site, which rises from A to a peak at B, the site of the 12th-century castle and the location of the main domestic buildings.

Symmetrical: Rectangular

Château de Vincennes

Vincennes in France had been the site of a royal hunting lodge since the 12th century, but redevelopment of the site in the late 14th century turned it into an enormous moated castle of rectilinear plan. An inset in one of the long sides of the bailey accommodates the 52-m (c.170-ft) high donjon, which contained the private apartments of the royal family. The square donjon has round corner towers and is set within its own moated square curtain, or chemise, with its own gateway.

While irregularity of plan was normal, more symmetrical and compact layouts were widely adopted from the 12th century onwards. An early example was the Louvre, the quadrangular castle begun in 1190 by Philip II Augustus outside the walls of Paris. (It is now reduced to its base, which is visible from within the Louvre museum beneath the Cour Carrée.) Several of the castles built for Edward I during his conquest of Wales in the late 13th century were built to symmetrical plans, including Flint and Beaumaris, both of which were rectangular. By the 14th century, quadrangular courtyard schemes had become an ideal for the builders of new castles.

Maxstoke Castle (plan)

Licensed in 1345, Maxstoke is an example
of a castle raised by an experienced soldier.
Its builder William de Clinton, Earl of
Huntingdon and veteran of the Hundred
Years War, chose a rectangular plan with
octagonal corner towers and a centrally
placed gatehouse. Despite Huntingdon's
military credentials, aesthetics played
a considerable part in the design.

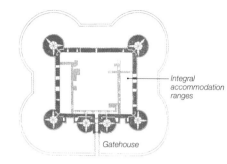

Château de Villandraut (plan)

Elected Pope in 1305, Clement V chose
a symmetrical form for his castle at
Villandraut – a rectangle with cylindrical
corner towers. Two similar towers flanked
the gateway, placed centrally in the south
front, which gave access to a quadrangular
courtyard around which the domestic
buildings were ranged.

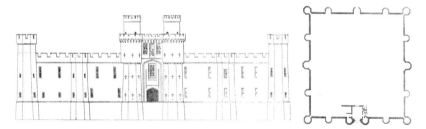

Herstmonceux Castle and plan

Built under licence in 1441, Herstmonceux
illustrates the degree to which symmetry
was taken in the design of late medieval
English castles. Constructed in brick, a
relatively unusual medium for English
castles at this time, the plan is a near-
square with octagonal corner towers and
regularly placed semi-octagonal interval
towers. The main façade was also designed
to produce a symmetrical appearance.
Slight discrepancies in the measurements
do little to detract from the overall impact
of regularity.

Symmetrical: Other Plans

While the rectangular plan was the most favoured for symmetrical design, owing to the practical advantages it offered for domestic planning, other figures were also used. One of the earliest was the octagonal plan of Castel del Monte in Puglia, Italy, built for the Holy Roman Emperor Frederick II from 1240. It is a masterpiece of military architecture. Such buildings gave castle builders the opportunity to use their geometrical knowledge and intellectual skills in creating an unusual, visually effective and practical design.

Pentagonal plan: Holt Castle

A highly unusual plan in the form of a regular pentagon was chosen for Holt Castle in Wales. Domestic accommodation was ranged around the inside of the curtain and there was a tower at each corner. The castle was probably built for John de Warrene, Earl of Surrey, in response to the renewal of war in Wales in 1282. It is possible that the King's masons were involved in the design. Holt Castle was demolished in the 17th century, but its character is known from pre-demolition drawings.

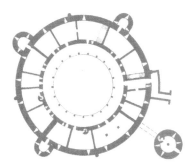

Circular: Bellver Castle (plan)

The early-14th-century royal castle of Bellver, near Palma, Mallorca, has a circular plan with protruding D-shaped towers at three of the cardinal points and a detached great tower at the fourth. Apartments are ranged around the interior of the curtain and the courtyard is surrounded by a two-storey loggia, which provides a shady retreat under which to sit or walk.

Concentric: Queenborough Castle (plan)

Queenborough, on the Isle of Sheppey in Kent, was built at the behest of Edward III by master mason John Box, in the 1360s. The castle's main block had a diameter of some 41.15 m (135 ft), just short of its counterpart at Bellver. In contrast to Bellver, Queenborough was given an outer bailey enclosed by a circular curtain wall and a moat, making it a concentric castle.

Queenborough Castle

Like Edward I's concentric castles in North Wales, the main block of Queenborough rose higher than the outer curtain and dominated the outer bailey. Regularly spaced round turrets projected from and climbed above the main block. Owing to the demolition of the castle in the 17th century, we cannot be certain of its internal arrangements, but it is likely that the principal accommodation was on the first floor of the main block.

Introduction

By the end of the Middle Ages, the castle as a military instrument had, to a great extent, become obsolete. Older castles that occupied strategic positions, and therefore retained a usefulness, were rendered vulnerable by improvements in artillery. The 17th century was a time of unrest in Europe and the castle suffered as a result. In England the Civil War of 1642–49 led to the demolition or 'slighting' of large numbers of castles by parliamentary decree. The devastating effect of the Civil War on castles was, to some degree, mirrored in the Central European wars of the 17th century, notably the Thirty Years War (1618–48), which also involved much destruction from the devastating power of gunpowder.

French Revolution: The Bastille

As a state prison and a hated symbol of royal oppression, the late-14th-century Bastille fell victim to the ire of the French revolutionaries. It was stormed on 14 July, 1789. Demolition began shortly after, and by the end of that year the building had been razed. The foundations of one of its towers was dug up in 1899 during the construction of the Metro, and re-erected in the Square Henri-Galli. Its outline is marked in the Place de la Bastille, but otherwise it has disappeared from view.

English Civil War: Bridgnorth Castle
The 12th-century keep of Bridgnorth
Castle, in Shropshire, was blown up by
parliamentarians in 1646 – a startling
testament to the violence inflicted on castles
during the English Civil War. In a state of
decay by the 16th century, the royalists use
of it as a garrison precipitated its demise.

English Civil War: Corfe Castle
Another casualty of the English Civil War
was Corfe Castle, in Dorset. One of the
few royalist strongholds in the region,
it was captured in 1645 and demolished
the following year with explosives. The
site and remains were used as a source
of building stone and timber.

Thirty Years War: Drachenfels Castle
Drachenfels sits above the Rhine, in Germany.
A castle of the Roman Catholic Archbishop
of Mainz, it was a natural target for the
Protestant Swedes who captured it during
the Thirty Years War. Though soon
recaptured, it was badly damaged and
was subsequently abandoned to quarrying.

Thirty Years War: Lahneck Castle
Another Rhineland castle of the Archbishop
of Mainz, Lahneck was built in the early
13th century. It was badly damaged by both
Protestant and Catholic forces during the
Thirty Years War, and was only refurbished
after passing into private hands in the
19th century.

Revival

Kronborg Castle
Kronborg Castle, in
Helsingør, Denmark, is
a Renaissance palace
that draws on the idea
of the medieval castle.
Begun in 1574, it was
built around an existing
15th-century castle.
Four symmetrically
arranged wings enclose
a rectangular courtyard,
and the four corner
towers, all quite different
in appearance, give an
asymmetrical look to
the elevations.

By the early 16th century the castle was defunct, but
the memory lingered and was to form a focus in the
wider Gothic revival movement. By the later 16th
century an interest in the medieval past had already
begun to manifest itself in secular architecture, and
the castle became a powerful influence on the character
of a great house, albeit in a decidedly contemporary
manner. In the 18th century the many ruined castles
that dotted the landscape were emulated by architects,
and in the 19th century, as scholarly knowledge of
Gothic architecture increased, so did a desire for
architectural authenticity in as far as it could be
accommodated in a modern house.

Lulworth Castle

Lulworth Castle, in Dorset, was completed in the early 17th century on an entirely new site. Its regular plan and projecting corner towers take their cue from quadrangular courtyard castles of the later Middle Ages. In fact, Lulworth has no courtyard, but originally a tower rose from the interior to suggest a keep surrounded by a curtain.

Bolsover Castle

Bolsover, in Derbyshire, is another 17th-century version of a castle, but built on the site of a former castle. The principal component of this tribute to the Middle Ages is the 'Little Castle', or keep, begun in 1612. Built to a square plan with a large stair turret at one corner, the Little Castle emulates medieval models.

Peckforton Castle

Few 19th-century castles are convincing, but Peckforton, in Cheshire, is a building with a truly medieval appearance. Built between 1844 and 1852, it is in a late-13th-century style, with particular reference to Caernarfon Castle, Edward I's masterpiece in North Wales.

Abbotsford House

By the early 19th century, emulation of the medieval castle had become part of the mainstream of domestic architecture. Walter Scott chose to build his house, Abbotsford, in a style dubbed 'Scottish Baronial' because it took its character from the late medieval castellated architecture.

Restoration

The revival of interest in the Middle Ages that inspired the design of new castellated buildings also prompted a reconsideration of surviving medieval castles. They might have been old-fashioned, dilapidated or ruinous, but they were authentic. With judicious improvements, or more drastic reinstatements, they might once again become fashionable and comfortable homes, with the added cachet of antiquity. Revitalisation of castles allowed old families to reassert their pedigree, new men to draw attention to their elevated positions and nations to remember their past.

Trakošcan Castle
Probably dating from the 13th century, Trakošcan Castle is in Croatia, close to the northern border with Slovenia. After several changes of tenure it was granted to the Draškovic family in 1584. Dilapidation followed a period of neglect in the 18th century, but the family reconstructed the castle in a romantic Neo-Gothic fashion from 1840–62, and created a landscaped park around it. The castle has a tactical position on a hill, but this adds to the romance of the 19th-century home it became.

Château de Pierrefonds, before restoration

Early drawings can assist in gauging the degree to which a castle has been restored. Pierrefonds, near Paris, was a ruin before reconstruction by Napoleon III. Drawings by the architect Viollet-le-Duc record the pre-restoration state of the castle.

Château de Pierrefonds, after restoration

A comparison of the pre-restoration drawing and one made post-restoration shows how much of the fabric is 19th rather than 14th century. A considerable proportion has been rebuilt and it is difficult to be certain of the degree to which the current building reflects its original character.

Hohenzollern Castle

The Hohenzollern family took its name from their 11th-century castle near Stuttgart, in Germany. One branch became the Prussian royal family, and Friedrich Wilhelm IV, King of Prussia, rebuilt Hohenzollern as a Neo-Gothic monument to them.

Wartburg Castle

Another 11th-century castle, Wartburg was the seat of the Landgraves of Thuringia, Germany, but fell into ruin in the post-medieval period. Its cultural associations, particularly with Martin Luther, were behind its restoration and large-scale reconstruction in the 19th century.

CASTLES **Feature by Feature**

Introduction

The great tower and the motte

There is a strong relationship between the great tower and the motte. Both dominated the castle with their height, and the motte was often surmounted by a tower, or acted as a revetment to a tower built up from ground level. Stone keeps were often built on top of an existing motte.

One of the most memorable aspects of the castle is the great tower, or keep, which usually formed part of the lord's lodgings. In France the great tower is usually known as the donjon, a name that derives from the Latin word for lord (dominus), which suggests that the donjon was particularly associated with lordship. In Spain the great tower is described as the *torre del homenaje* (tower of homage), which reflects the practice in medieval feudal society of rendering an homage to a lord. In England the terms 'great tower', 'donjon' and 'keep' are used interchangeably.

Additional keeps

Occasionally a castle has more than one great tower. During the 15th century, while adding to the residential accommodation of the Alcázar of Segovia, in central Spain, King Juan II of Castille built a second keep at the opposite end of the castle from the existing great tower.

Converted elements

The great tower was not always an original component of a castle. Some enclosure castles had keeps added to them at a later date. At Richmond Castle, in North Yorkshire, the 12th-century keep was raised on the site of the 11th-century gatehouse, incorporating parts of the gatehouse in its build.

Battered plinth

An echo of the motte is to be found in the splayed, or battered, base of Conisbrough Castle keep, in South Yorkshire, which contains the basement of the tower. This thicker lower wall, reducing in thickness up to first-floor level, gives the keep greater structural stability.

Shell Keep

The polygonal plan
Many shell keeps are polygonal in plan. This was a reasonable solution to the problems posed by the physical characteristics of the site. At Lincoln Castle, in Lincolnshire, the 12th-century shell keep that crowns one of the two mottes has 15 faces demarcated by pilaster buttresses.

Although the timber superstructures of motte and bailey castles have long since disappeared, pictorial and archaeological evidence suggests that the tops of mottes were invariably encircled by a timber palisade, which sometimes enclosed a tower or other buildings. When a motte and bailey castle came to be rebuilt in stone this palisade was replaced by a stone perimeter wall. Such constructions are known as 'shell keeps', although they are really enclosures rather than keeps. Most date from the 11th and 12th centuries, but many were adapted in later periods.

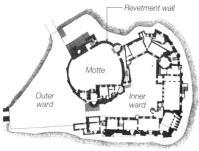

Revetment wall

Motte

Outer ward

Inner ward

The revetment

Most shell keeps were constructed on top of the motte. but in a few instances they are upward extensions of the stone cladding of a motte. One such example is at Berkeley Castle. in Gloucestershire. where the 12th-century remodelling of the castle included the revetment of the motte.

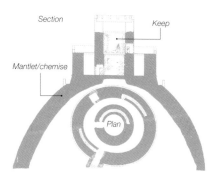

Section

Keep

Mantlet/chemise

Plan

The mantlet or chemise (plan)

Sometimes there is a combination of shell keep and tower keep, as at Launceston Castle. in Cornwall. Here the 12th-century tower is surrounded by a 13th-century wall. which. had it been on its own. would be called a shell keep. In these circumstances. however. it is better referred to as a mantlet or chemise.

The lord's residence

There is plenty of evidence to show that the shell keep often contained the lord's apartments. Few such complexes survive. but the shell keep of Tamworth Castle. in Staffordshire. remained inhabited until the end of the 19th century. and retains the 15th-century. timber-framed great hall among the surviving medieval buildings.

Hall Keep

Hall keep proportions
An 11th-century
example of a hall keep
is at Colchester Castle,
in Essex. It was begun in
the 1070s. Shown from
the north-east, the keep
has a squat appearance
quite at odds with the
proportions of tower
keeps generally.
It contained two main
storeys, with similar
accommodation in
each focused on a hall.

An antecedent of the keep is the medieval hall, raised
to first-floor level for security purposes. A recognisable
development of the raised hall is the hall keep. Low in
relation to its lateral dimensions, this form resulted
in a comparatively squat building. A structure of
greater substance might be created by building two
such blocks side by side in order to increase the range
of accommodation. Hall keeps are generally two- or
three-storey, though some have been raised at later
dates and converted into tower keeps.

Hall keep main entrance

The main entrance to Colchester was at ground-floor level, although this storey was substantially raised as the keep was built on top of the vaulted podium of a Roman temple. The entrance is up against one of the corner turrets, which contains the main staircase giving access to the upper storey.

Staircase   *Entrance*   *Apse*   *Hall*

Hall keep ground-floor (plan)

Colchester's ground-floor entrance opened to a lobby, allowing independent access to the ground and first-floor suites via a staircase. The unusual plan created by the apsidal projection has a striking resemblance to the Tower of London's White Tower, of similar date. Both were probably influenced by continental antecedents.

Hall keep

Hall keeps continued to be built into the 12th century. An example is Castle Rising, in Norfolk, dating from c.1140. A highly decorated forebuilding stood in front of this palatial residence. In it, a grand staircase led to a first-floor vestibule before the great hall, which occupied one side of the main block.

Tower Keep

Early tower keep

The donjon of Château de Loches, in the Loire Valley in France, was raised in the early 11th century. It rises through four storeys to over 30 m (100 ft). A tall basement, lit by narrow security loops high up in the walls, supported three upper storeys of high-quality residential accommodation. Two views of the donjon are shown here.

A slightly later development is the tower keep, a building that rose through at least three storeys, and often more. The earliest tower keeps date from the 11th century, and the form remained a staple of castle architecture throughout the medieval period. Then, as now, patrons and architects favoured height to create an architectural effect, and most tower keeps should probably be looked upon as prestige residences. There is no doubt that they were secure dwellings, but there was no particular defensive advantage in building ever higher.

The optical illusion

Occasionally the desire for height surpassed the need for accommodation. Externally, the keep of Hedingham Castle, in Essex, appears to have five storeys, but, as built, it had only three: a basement, a lower hall and a tall upper hall with a fenestrated gallery. The 'fourth and fifth' storeys were, in fact, a wall pierced with false windows screening the roof.

The detached tower keep

In a few cases the great tower is emphasised by being placed outside the enceinte, close to the entrance, like the *torre del homenaje* of Bellver Castle near Palma, Mallorca. The tower dominates the castle's profile from a distance, holding visitors' attention until they reach the gateway.

The hilltop keep

The natural environment could be used to help in achieving height. At hill sites like that of Château de Landskron in Alsace, France, the great tower was placed at the apex of the site, a move that enhanced not only its verticality and dramatic effect, but also its visual reach.

Forebuilding

The entrance to a great tower was often protected by a forebuilding. This acted as a porch and also protected the staircase, as the entrance to the great tower proper was usually at an upper-floor level. The forebuilding was a relatively early development. The early-11th-century donjon of Château de Loches, in the Loire Valley, France, for example, was provided with one from the start. Its forebuilding originally extended to the full height of the donjon, but they were usually lower than the main building.

The integrated forebuilding
In some cases the forebuilding is masked through integration with the keep. At the early-12th-century great tower of Arques-la-Bataille, in Normandy, France, the forebuilding begins as a single-storey structure on the main front (beneath the right-hand arch), and then wraps around the corner of the building and rises to full height.

Donjon section

At the corner of the Arques donjon was a second door opening to a vestibule at the foot of a staircase. A long straight flight of steps ascended directly to the second floor landing, where a doorway opened to an entrance hall. This landing was protected by murder holes in the floor above.

The porch

Sometimes the forebuilding was more of a porch than a defensive outwork. Orford Castle, in Suffolk, is a non-military building dating from the 1160s. The low forebuilding of its keep is situated in the angle between the main block and one of three projecting turrets. It contains a prison cell at basement level, a first-floor entrance lobby and a second-floor chapel.

The chapel

In a number of instances the forebuilding housed a chapel. At Newcastle, the ground storey of the forebuilding, which extends across the full length of the late-12th-century keep, was entirely occupied by the castle chapel. A gateway tower next to the chapel entrance gave access to a grand stair that led to the second-floor main entrance.

Cylindrical Keep

Although the first great towers were rectangular in plan, other forms followed, the most popular being the cylindrical keep. One of the earliest is at Château de Fréteval in the Loire Valley, France, which may date from the late 11th century. The earliest in England is at New Buckenham Castle, in Suffolk, which probably dates from c.1140. The adoption of the cylindrical form is often attributed to its greater structural stability and deflectional qualities, which helped protect against both mining and missiles. Fashion probably also played its part in the adoption of cylindrical keeps.

Château de Coucy
The greatest of all cylindrical donjons was that of the c.1220 Château de Coucy, in Picardy, France. Rising to a height of c.60 m (200 ft), it was over 30 m (100 ft) in diameter, and the wall was 7-m (23-ft) thick at ground level. All three storeys were covered in high rib vaults. The structure exuded wealth, power and authority.

Ground floor (plan)

Access to Coucy's donjon was from the inner courtyard via a bridge that spanned the surrounding ditch. The entrance passage, which was protected by a portcullis, two doors and an iron grill, communicated with a latrine (left), a staircase leading to the upper storeys (right), and a ground-floor chamber equipped with a well and a fireplace.

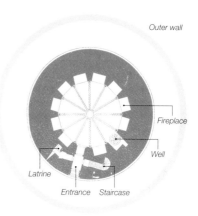

Outer wall

Fireplace

Well

Latrine

Entrance   Staircase

Outer wall

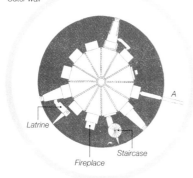

A

Latrine

Staircase

Fireplace

First-floor (plan)

A spiral staircase ascended to first-floor level at Coucy, where there was a single chamber equipped with a fireplace and latrine. A postern gate (A) within one of the recesses allowed access to and from the chemise wall that enclosed the allure (wall walk) of the surrounding ditch.

Second-floor (plan)

Coucy's second floor contained the grandest room of all. Some 3 m (10 ft) above the level of the central chamber, a mural gallery gave access to wooden balconies fitted within the recesses that extended around the room. The room probably functioned as a ceremonial assembly hall and these balconies would have been for the spectators.

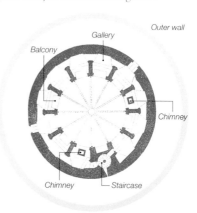

Outer wall

Gallery

Balcony

Chimney

Chimney   Staircase

Cylindrical Variants

Conisbrough Castle
The late 12th-century keep at Conisbrough Castle, in Yorkshire, is a sophisticated variant of the cylindrical tower. It has six semi-polygonal turrets disposed symmetrically around the circumference. These are largely solid, and could have been defensive, structural or aesthetic in intent.

For anyone accustomed to the tradition of the rectangular keep, the cylindrical design must have seemed revolutionary. Great towers of unmodified circular plan were built in considerable numbers, but in other cases the circular basis was varied with the addition of turrets. Such adjuncts were useful in providing space for mural chambers, although only occasionally does this seem to have been a prime consideration. It may be that some builders found the lack of orientation in the cylindrical form disconcerting, or felt the need to relieve the monotony of the elevation.

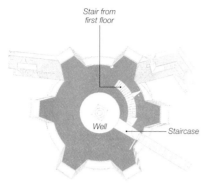

Ground floor (plan)

Entry was at first-floor level, to a plain room with a hole in the centre of the stone-paved floor giving access to a well in the vaulted basement below. There is no other access to the basement, which must have served as a storage area.

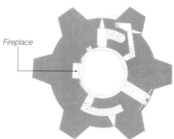

First-floor (plan)

From the entrance passage, a mural staircase led to one large residential room. It had a hooded fireplace and a passage leading to a mural garderobe. Another staircase, off one of the window embrasures, gave access to the upper storey and roof.

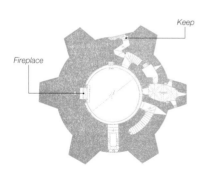

Second-floor (plan)

At second-floor level was another large chamber equipped with fireplace and garderobe, and, in one of the turrets, a chapel. From the main room another staircase led to the roof.

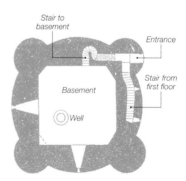

Château de Houdan (plan)

An early-12th-century, and transitional example is at Château de Houdan, near Paris. Four semi-circular turrets project from the cardinal points of the tower, but the interior of the main block is rectangular.

Quatrefoil Keep

The quatrefoil was another design based on the circle. The geometrical source of the plan is four intersecting circles resulting in a symmetrical cluster of four prominent lobes. The main example of this type is the mid-12th-century donjon known as the Tour de Guinette in the royal Château d'Étampes, in northern France. This is now an isolated building, but was originally surrounded by a chemise. The quatrefoil form was both an aesthetic novelty, and a building that shared the defensive qualities of the cylindrical donjon.

Elevation
The visual impact of the donjon is suggested by this reconstruction drawing (based partly on a drawing of the castle in a 15th-century manuscript). Access to the donjon was via a drawbridge from the surrounding chemise to an entrance set between two of the lobes, something in the manner of a twin-towered gatehouse.

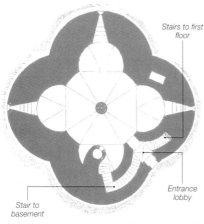

Basement (plan)

The donjon was entered midway between basement and first-floor levels. The entrance passage opened to a vaulted lobby giving access to stairs that led to both basement and first floor, before continuing to an opening approximately 3.5 m (12 ft) above the basement floor. The basement contained a well and was lit by loops in each of the four lobes.

First-floor (plan)

The principal feature of the first-floor room was its high ribbed vault, which was supported on a central column. A latrine opened off one of the lobes, but there is no sign of a fireplace, and it is possible that this room was more of an audience chamber or assembly hall than a living room.

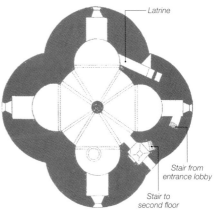

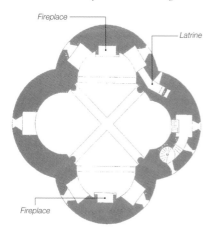

Second-floor (plan)

The main living accommodation was at second-floor level, where, in contrast to the apparent spartan character of the first-floor chamber, there were two fireplaces as well as a latrine. This room was also vaulted, with four ribs springing from engaged shafts with capitals.

Polygonal Keep

During the 12th century and later, a number of great towers were built to polygonal plans. An early example is Caesar's Tower at Provins, in northern France, which is based on a regular octagon. It is doubtful that there was any particular military advantage to this form, and probable that the main attraction was architectural. The donjon was built on top of a revetted motte, the revetment being carried up to form a chemise wall around Caesar's Tower.

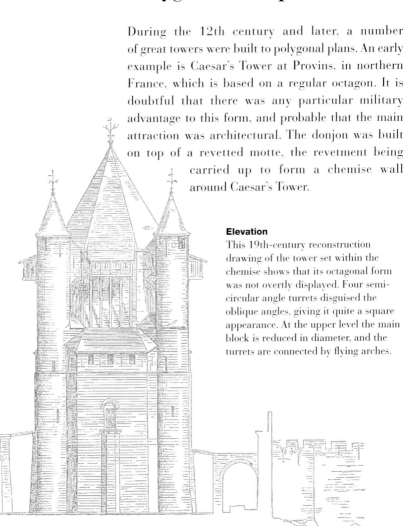

Elevation

This 19th-century reconstruction drawing of the tower set within the chemise shows that its octagonal form was not overtly displayed. Four semi-circular angle turrets disguised the oblique angles, giving it quite a square appearance. At the upper level the main block is reduced in diameter, and the turrets are connected by flying arches.

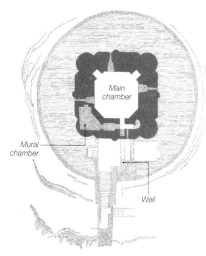

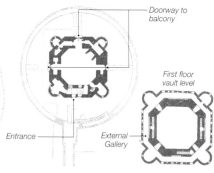

Ground floor (plan)

There was no external access to the ground floor, which was reached via a staircase from the first floor. This led to an entrance passage, which communicated with a staircase descending to a well. The main chamber was nearly square, with short diagonals at the corners. In one corner was a mural chamber, possibly a prison.

First-floor (plan)

Access to the tower was at first-floor level from the west, via a drawbridge from the allure of the chemise. A high-vaulted central room was supplemented with small mural chambers. Doorways in the centre of north, south and east sides led to balconies.

Gallery

A staircase led from the first floor to an external gallery that extended all around the tower at the level from which the vault of the first-floor room sprang. The central first-floor room was illuminated from gallery level. Stairs led from here to an upper storey and roof.

111

Tower House

Tower house is a name given to great towers that are self-contained dwellings. The name is usually applied to smaller towers built by the lesser nobility in unsettled regions in which the characteristic form of residence was a tower. It is not generally applied to the great towers that form part of a castle. However, some great towers were as self-contained as tower houses, and some buildings that are described as tower houses form elements of wider complexes. The term is therefore used in an imprecise fashion, and there is no universally accepted definition.

Mini castles

In effect, the tower house was a mini castle compressed into a single, easily defendable unit, with the principal living area placed securely in an upper floor. Sometimes the tower house had corner turrets that aped the corner towers of courtyard castles: usually it had a defended entrance and a crenellated parapet, which was often machicolated.

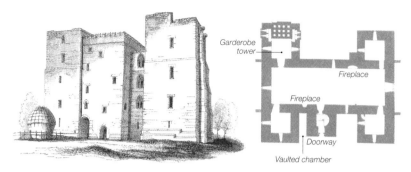

England: Langley Castle with plan

The outbreak of war between England and Scotland in 1297 initiated a 300-year period of insecurity and a proliferation of fortification in both countries. Langley Castle, in Northumberland, is an example of a 13th-century manor house that was converted into a tower in the mid-14th century, probably as a response to the deterioration in the level of security.

Scotland: Borthwick

Borthwick, near Edinburgh, which dates from c.1430, was built as a tower from the outset. However, the design of the four-storey building has, at its nucleus, a first-floor hall occupying the main body of the building .

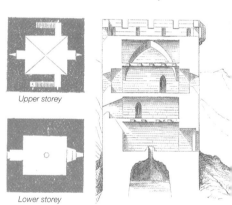

Syria: Tukhlah

A number of 12th-century tower houses existed in the Crusader states. At Tukhlah, in Syria, a square, battlemented tower, with an entrance protected by machicolation, contained a water cistern in the basement and two vaulted storeys, each sub-divided by wooden floors.

Solar Tower

The solar tower and the hall

Where both buildings survive, the dependent relationship of the solar tower to the great hall is usually apparent. The great hall, with its large floor area, was a room for communal living, while the solar tower, with its more compact plan and greater height, implies a more personal space for an important personage.

Whereas the tower house was a self-contained building, another type of residential tower, known as the solar tower, was one element of a more extensive domestic complex. 'Solar' was a word used in the medieval period to describe a private room on an upper floor. Solar towers contained the private apartments of the lord and were associated with a separate great hall. The term 'solar tower', like 'tower house', is a modern classification. During the medieval period it is unlikely that either type would have been distinguished from the broad tradition of the great tower.

Stokesay Castle

Like other great towers, the solar tower was usually the architectural climax of a wider complex and the masterpiece that advertised the owner's wealth and status. The highly unusual plan of the solar tower of Stokesay Castle, in Shropshire, was probably influenced by contemporary works on the royal castles of North Wales. It was built in the 1280s or 1290s.

Mortham Tower

Sometimes, while the tower itself survives, the surrounding buildings were replaced over the centuries, so the accompanying complex is of a later date. Such is the case at Mortham Hall, in North Yorkshire, where the 15th-century tower, with its polygonal bartizans and unusual openwork parapet, rises above the replacement buildings.

Tattershall

Where accompanying buildings have been destroyed, the solar tower occasionally survives, giving it the appearance of an isolated great tower. At Tattershall Castle, in Lincolnshire, the solar tower of 1434–1446 was formerly linked to subsidiary buildings, including a great hall and kitchen, by covered passages.

Later Great Towers

The great tower was a secure building that acted as a useful vantage point and sometimes as a refuge of last resort, but there is no doubt that it also had the capacity to provide an impressive and extensive lordly residence. During the later medieval period, the great tower was the focus of numerous residential schemes. Some of these blurred the distinction of the architectural form, while still retaining the concept of the great tower as a symbol of lordship. It was during this period that the great tower reached the acme of its architectural potential.

Perspective: Château de Pierrefonds

In some instances, the donjon formed the palatial centrepiece of a courtyard complex, as at Pierrefonds, near Paris. The donjon of

c.1400 dominated the inner courtyard and rose above the adjacent apartments. The vaulted ground storey of Pierrefonds was given over to storage.

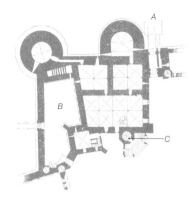

Ground-floor: Château de Pierrefonds (plan)

Sited between the main gateway (A) and a service yard (B), the donjon is integrated with the curtain and wall towers. Access to the residential rooms was via a polygonal stair turret (C).

First-floor: Château de Pierrefonds (plan)

The main staircase led to a large first-floor suite comprising a hall (A), two smaller chambers beyond that (B), and further rooms situated in the two wall towers and over the adjacent gateway (C). A similar suite occupied the second floor.

Third-floor: Château de Pierrefonds (plan)

Further residential accommodation was found at third-floor level, and here there was also access to two machicolated allures (A and B). Staircases in turrets at the two corners of the great tower, leading to the roof and battlements, were accessible from the main room.

Introduction

In its simplest form, the curtain is a wall with a crenellated parapet, possibly pierced with arrow loops, but uninterrupted by towers and other adjuncts. It was a reasonably efficient way of controlling access to the lord and of securing his possessions, but possibly less effective against siege engines.

Although the great tower was the most impressive element of the castle, the enceinte was more fundamental to its defence. Enceinte was the name given to the continuous circuit of fortifications that formed the enclosure, and is used to describe not only the curtain wall and its various adjuncts and embellishments, but also other encircling features, including ditches and moats. Simple in its early manifestations, the enceinte developed considerably under the impetus of improvements in siege warfare techniques, reaching its military apogee in the 13th century.

Defensive wall towers

The addition of projecting wall towers allowed flanking fire to be directed along the face of the curtain. Systematic deployment of defensive wall towers began during the second half of the 12th century. One of the prime examples in England is Framlingham Castle, in Suffolk, which was rebuilt c.1190 with 13 projecting square wall towers.

Closely spaced towers

An innovation in the disposition of wall towers was introduced in the 1230s at Angers Castle, in the Loire Valley, France. A new curtain wall was built with 17 cylindrical towers much closer together than in earlier castles. This provided the inhabitants with a more formidable line of defence.

Beaked towers

The development of wall towers in the 13th century centred on the formulation of less structurally vulnerable forms than the rectangle. Cylindrical towers were less susceptible to mining than the earlier rectangular towers, and the beaked form shown here, which was deployed at Château de Loches in the early 13th century, deflected missiles more effectively.

Batter or Talus

Krak des Chevaliers
One of the most impressive examples of a medieval talus is the one at the Hospitaller castle of Krak des Chevaliers, in Syria. This feature, which is shown here from the south-east, extended around the south and west sides of the inner enceinte, encompassing the bases of the wall towers which were thus protected.

The batter was a thickening of the wall base to make an inclined plane; an exaggerated form of batter was the talus. These features were advantageous in several ways. Firstly, they gave protection against mining, in that the broader base gave the wall greater stability. Secondly, they made scaling the wall more difficult because the engines used were kept at a distance by the protruding base of the wall. Thirdly, the increased thickness that the talus gave to the curtain provided greater protection against missiles. Finally, their deflective qualities could be used as part of an aggressive defence, with missiles dropped from above being propelled from them towards the besiegers.

120

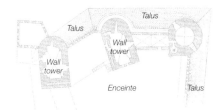

Krak des Chevaliers (plan)

The plan of the south end of the inner enceinte of Krak des Chevaliers emphasises the extra depth the great talus gave to the curtain. It brings the foot of the curtain in line with, or considerably beyond, the faces of the adjacent projecting wall towers.

Kidwelly

A special kind of batter was developed during the 13th century for round or polygonal towers. It involved building on a larger, square foundation, the outer corners of which were carried up on inclined planes to clutch the tower. These angle batters are known as 'spurs'.

Caesarea Palace

Although the palace of Caesarea, in Israel, has been largely destroyed, the better-preserved defences of the attached town retain a good example of the talus, which extended up to the foot of a gallery pierced with arrow loops.

Castle of La Mota

From the 15th century, castle defences were strengthened to counter the use of artillery in siege warfare. The castle of La Mota, in Medina del Campo, central Spain, was reconstructed in the mid-15th century, adding an exaggerated batter to the outer curtain with the object of absorbing the impact of cannon fire.

Great Tower

While the great tower was always a popular component of the castle, the emphasis on the curtain, which dominated the development of the European castle during the late 12th and 13th centuries, was accompanied by a loosening of the concept of the great tower as a stand-alone structure. In some of the castles in which the great tower was retained, it became a more integral part of the outer defences, while still maintaining its special status as the lord's tower.

The solitary wall tower
Occasionally the great tower is the only wall tower, as at the late-14th-century Château de Vez in Picardy, France. Here, the pentagonal great tower is sited at one of the angles of a lightly defended, roughly quadrangular enclosure. This asymmetrical arrangement is in direct contrast to another trend of the later Middle Ages towards regularly planned courtyard castles.

The integral corner tower (plan)

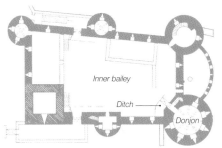

A more integrated approach was taken in the mid-13th century at Château de Najac, in the Aveyron, in the south of France. At Najac, the donjon, which again acts as one of the corner towers, is attached to the curtain, though it had a degree of isolation in being separated from the bailey by a ditch.

The detached corner tower (plan)

In some cases the great tower maintained its independence by remaining detached while still forming part of the enceinte. At Flint Castle, in North Wales, Edward I's keep, begun in 1277, took the form of an enlarged corner tower, albeit detached from the curtain and connected to it by a bridge.

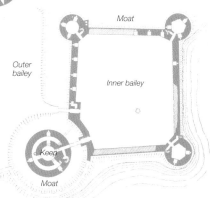

A justiciar's lodging

Despite the impression of uniformity among the wall towers of Caernarvon Castle, the Eagle Tower was, in fact, larger and more prominent than the others. It served a particular function: it was probably built to house the Justiciar of North Wales. Like other great towers, it has a strong association with lordship and authority.

Ditches & Moats

Protective ditches and their accompanying earthen banks are among the oldest type of defence, with a pedigree stretching back to before the time of written records. Most early castles were enclosed by a bank and ditch, the excavated material from the ditch being thrown up to create the surrounding bank and/or to build up the platform of the enclosure. The ditch gave the castle defenders a military edge by allowing them to tower above anyone who tried to approach the walls rather than the gate; it also prevented siege machines from coming too close.

The stream-filled moat
With inland sites, the water source for a moat was often a spring or stream. At Saint-Médard-en-Jalles, in the Gironde, in south-west France, the fortified manor house was built on the right bank of a river, and the moat around it was fed by the stream.

The rock-cut ditch

An effective way of protecting a promontory castle was to cut a ditch through the line of approach. An extreme example of such an operation was carried out at Saone Castle, in Syria. A massive ditch was hewn through the rock with just one pillar left in the centre, allowing the 18-m (60-ft) wide ditch to be bridged.

Earthworks

The earthworks of early castles were generally so substantial that they were retained throughout the life of the castle. This is the case at Arques-la-Bataille, near Dieppe, in France. The basis of its earlier defensive system was a surrounding ditch and bank and these, despite later rebuilding in stone, still define the extent of the existing castle.

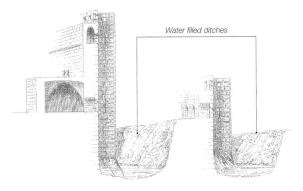

Water filled ditches

The sea-filled moat

If there was a reliable source of water, the ditch might be flooded to provide a further obstacle. A water supply posed no problem at the 12th-century coastal Castle of Tortosa, in Syria. The double water-filled ditch was fed by the sea.

Extended Water Defences

Leeds Castle
Leeds Castle, in Kent, is surrounded by a large lake, created by damming the adjacent River Len. The late-13th-century castle, which was used as a royal retreat, was at the centre of a planned landscape, including the lake. This enhanced both the castle's landscape setting and its leisure facilities.

Water defences were a highly effective way of excluding trespassers and keeping a besieging army at bay. They made mining impossible and prevented men and siege engines from coming close to the curtain, thus making attack by escalade impractical. The greater the barrier, the more effective its defensive properties, so water defences could be very extensive wherever the natural sources and topography made this possible. Moats enhanced defence, but there is also reason to suppose that some might have been designed to improve the visual setting of the castle.

Chillon Castle

Chillon Castle, in Switzerland, was substantially remodelled by Count Peter II of Savoy in the 13th century. It is situated on an island close to the east bank of Lake Geneva. The lake forms a natural defence, particularly on the western side, where the plain curtain wall was considered to be adequate protection.

Caerphilly Castle (plan)

Where a natural lake did not exist, one could be created. The water defences of Caerphilly Castle, in Glamorgan, Wales, formed part of one of the most elaborate 13th-century castle defence systems. The final extent of the scheme does not seem to have been contemplated from the outset, but rather developed in a number of stages.

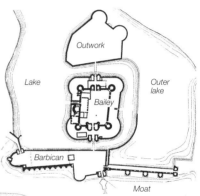

Bodiam Castle (plan)

Sometimes a surviving castle moat is the remnant of a greater complex of water features. The broad moat that surrounds Bodiam Castle, in Sussex, plays a prominent part in the castle's impact on the landscape, but originally there were several other water features, which were probably intended to contribute to the landscape setting.

Introduction

Château de Coucy
The 13th-century north-west corner tower at Château de Coucy, in Picardy, France, performed both defensive and residential functions. The battered base, alternating arrow loops and hoarding all attest to its military aspect, but some of the rooms were also equipped with a view to domestic occupation.

Towers other than the great tower also made a major contribution to the castle. From the 11th century onwards, these were built at intervals along the curtain wall. Like great towers, the earliest wall towers were rectangular in plan, but from the 12th century they were also being built to circular or D-shaped plans. These forms allowed a more comprehensive field of fire and were less vulnerable to attack from mining. Wall towers might also contain domestic accommodation. Turrets were lesser structures that might intersperse wall towers or augment a larger tower, while bartizans provided vantage points at parapet level.

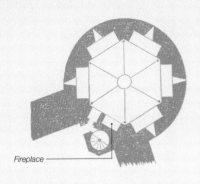

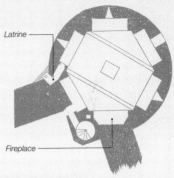

Latrine

Fireplace

Fireplace

First-floor (plan)

Coucy's first floor has a hexagonal plan and is covered by a vault carried on six ribs. The five faces of the hexagon pointing towards the exterior each contained an arrow loop. A fireplace in the only interior face provided a degree of comfort.

Second-floor (plan)

At second-floor level the positions of the loops alternate with those of the first floor, so that only four sides correspond with the exterior face of the tower. Here, there is both a fireplace and a latrine.

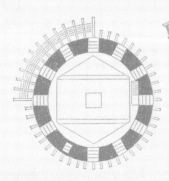

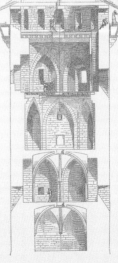

Battlement (plan)

The fourth floor at Coucy is a fighting platform from which access to the surrounding hoarding can be gained and the main defence of the tower conducted. This storey could only be reached by a removable ladder.

Section

An interesting aspect of Coucy's tower is the provision made for hauling materials between floors – openings in the centres of the vaults. The lowest storey was accessible only from such an opening in the vault.

Defensive Towers

The curtain wall provided a basic level of defence, but the provision of towers along its length added greatly to its capabilities. Wall towers, which rose above and projected outside the curtain, had two military advantages: they offered vantage points for observation, and they allowed the base of the curtain to be defended more effectively by supplying positions from which to conduct flanking fire along its face. In early castles wall towers were comparatively few, but their tactical significance came to be increasingly appreciated.

Open-backed towers
Defensive towers were often open-backed, like this 14th-century example at The Popes' Palace at Avignon, in the south of France. The design was economical and practical. Without the encumbrance of a domestic layout, it facilitated the free movement of personnel.

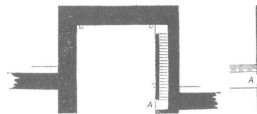

Ground floor (plan)

Access to the tower of the Popes' Palace was at ground level, where a door (A) opened to a straight mural staircase ascending to the first-floor platform.

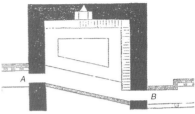

First-floor (plan)

At first-floor level, the allure of the adjacent curtain extends through the tower via entrances in the two side walls (A and B). In the outer wall there is an arrow loop, and a second staircase leads from the allure to parapet level.

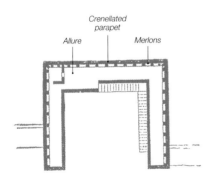

Second-floor (plan)

At the top of the tower is a broad allure with a crenellated parapet around the three sides, the merlons being pierced by arrow loops. The tower would have been roofed to give protection from the elements.

Arrow loops

One of the functions of defensive wall towers was to provide additional space for arrow loops. Rounded towers like this one were designed with whole tiers of arrow loops, giving them a very wide field of fire.

Lodging Towers

Although towers were originally defensive features, a factor reflected in the entirely military character of some surviving examples, it was swiftly understood that their usefulness would be greatly increased if they also provided accommodation, either for storage or for habitation. By the 11th century, wall towers were being utilised to perform a variety of functions, and by the 14th century the growing need for good-quality residential lodgings resulted in towers whose principal purpose was domestic.

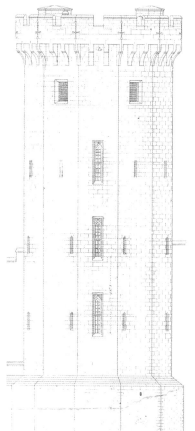

Guy's Tower, Warwick Castle

Guy's Tower, a late 14th-century 12-sided building in the north angle of Warwick Castle, in Warwickshire, has a machicolated and crenellated parapet. This allows for its defence, but, like many wall towers of the later Middle Ages, its main purpose was to provide high-quality accommodation for important guests and officials. This is suggested by the good-quality window tracery of the three middle storeys. The top storey, with its wide windows, was not residential; it may have served as an observation post or belvedere.

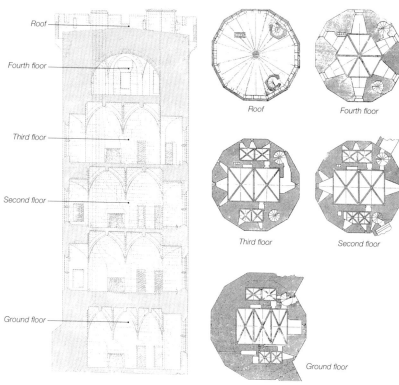

Roof

Fourth floor

Third floor

Second floor

Ground floor

Roof

Fourth floor

Third floor

Second floor

Ground floor

Section

The tower contains four individual
lodgings, one above the other, each with
a fireplace, a latrine and a small private
mural chamber. Each of the main rooms
was covered with a ribbed vault. Three of
these lodgings were quite clearly intended
for occupants ranking relatively high in the
social scale, the basement lodging being
slightly less commodious owing to a lack
of fenestration towards the exterior.

Floor plans

All four lodgings were entered from the
same spiral staircase. Despite the polygonal
exterior of the tower, the main rooms were
rectangular, a more practical shape for
domestic living, but perhaps also designed
to allow space for the latrines and private
chambers. The fact that the mural chambers
have rib vaults rather than less costly barrel
vaults also attests to the high quality of the
rooms. A second staircase led to the roof.

133

Turrets

Wall towers improved the defensive capability of the curtain by providing forward positions from which the face of the wall might be enfiladed. Increasingly, they came to have a residential function as well, and in later castles this eclipsed their military role. The purely defensive aspect of the wall tower, however, could be fulfilled by mid-wall turrets, which were much cheaper to build. Whereas wall towers might soar above the curtain, the smaller turrets were essentially wallhead defences providing strategically placed points of tactical advantage.

Machicolated turret: Avignon
This mid-wall turret at Avignon in the south of France allowed a vantage point slightly higher than the allure, thus providing the curtain with an extra level of protection over the battered plinth and machicolations. Protection of the turret itself was provided by the heavily machicolated parapet.

Corbelled turret: Vez (left)

Examples that are similar in principle, though simpler and more lightly defended, also exist. This late-14th-century instance at Vez in northern France is simply a projection of the line of the curtain supported on corbelling. Although the parapet is pierced with arrow loops, there is no machicolation and it has something of an ornamental appearance.

Turret section (above)

Efforts were made to reduce the vulnerability of the Avignon turret, in this case by integrating its supports with the deeply battered plinth so that it could not be undermined without great difficulty. In addition to the corbelled machicolations (A) it also had a slot machicolation to the rear (B).

Turret to rear

The Avignon turret was reached from the allure by two flights of steps. The allure itself was uninterrupted: it continued beneath a covered gallery, the roof of which served as part of the platform associated with the turret.

Bartizans

Bartizans and corbels

Circular bartizans on continuous corbelled bands were in vogue in Scotland and the north of England from the 14th century onwards. Those at Belsay Castle, in Northumberland, date from c.1370, but 13th-century examples also exist. Belsay has machicolated bartizans, which allows them to perform a defensive function as well as an ornamental one.

During the 13th century, a form of turret known as the bartizan was developed. This feature projects from, and is entirely supported by, the castle wall, and so overhangs the wall face. Bartizans perform one of the functions of turrets in providing vantage points from which the face of a wall might be perused or enfiladed. They have a military advantage because, having no foundations, they cannot be undermined. While some early bartizans extend a long way down the face of the wall, in the later Middle Ages, bartizans were mostly found at parapet height, particularly at angles.

Circular bartizans

Many bartizans had a circular plan because the shape worked well at a corner. This example, from the Château Comtal in Carcassonne, southern France, is supported on tiered corbels projecting from the two adjacent faces of the wall. The corbels support curved lintels, and a line of continuous corbelling sits on the lintels.

Bartizans and turrets

The late medieval bartizan has much in common with the corbelled turret. Structural principles are similar, the main difference being one of scale, so that these examples at the Popes' Palace at Avignon, in the south of France, might be described as elongated bartizans.

Ornamental bartizans

Circular bartizans on continuous corbelling continued to be popular during the 15th century in France and Scotland. Later examples, as at Château de Sédières, in south-west France, were more exaggerated than their earlier counterparts, thus becoming purely ornamental.

Wallhead Defence

The allure

The allure usually took the form of a stone-paved walkway flanked on one side by a crenellated parapet, the merlons of which were often pierced by arrow loops. In the late medieval period some curtain walls had a crenellated parapet on the inner side as well as the outer.

Much of the defence of a castle was conducted from the wallhead, a position that provided the defenders with great tactical advantages, and one that received a good deal of attention from military engineers. The main artery of wallhead defence was a walkway along the top of the wall known as the allure. Protected by a parapet, the allure was an essential route of communication by which the defences might be manned and supplied. It also acted as a vantage point from which movement in the surrounding countryside could be monitored.

Guardroom: Carcassone (plan)

Occasionally, accommodation for the guards who patrolled the walls can be identified, as in this example from Carcassonne, in the south of France. The allure passes through a wall turret that projects from each side of the curtain and so gives a little more space than can be found on the allure.

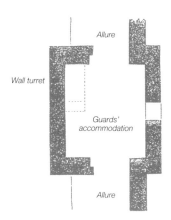

Allure

Wall turret

Guards' accommodation

Allure

Guardroom section: Carcassone

The Carcassonne guardroom contained a fireplace set against the inner wall of the turret, with a stone hood above it. It is also clear that this area was roofed and fitted with doors. The result is a facility in which the guards might warm themselves in cold weather while maintaining their watch from a loop in the outer wall.

Château de Tarascon

A late-14th-century innovation in castle design was the construction of towers and curtain of the same height so that there was an uninterrupted allure. One such scheme survives in the south of France at Tarascon, on the banks of the Rhône. It was begun in 1400. Aside from its defensive considerations, it creates a quite different aesthetic.

Battlements

Castle parapets were invariably crenellated: indeed,
crenellation was one of the features by which a castle
might be formally identified as a fortification.
In England, royal sanction of a castle came in the form
of a licence to crenellate, the wording of which
invariably makes clear that, in official terms,
crenellation equalled fortification. While battlements
were a practical aspect of defence, there was also an
element of fashion in crenellation, and possibly
symbolism as well in that it denoted nobility.

Stepped battlements
The crenellated parapet
protected the entire circuit
of the allure. Where there
were alterations in the level
of the walkway, this had
to be compensated for with
a corresponding change in
the parapet. Thus, where
steps are encountered the
parapet was also stepped to
maintain the correct height.

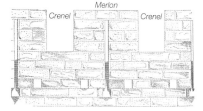

Exterior view

Merlon

Crenel · Crenel

Interior view

Arrow loop

Allure

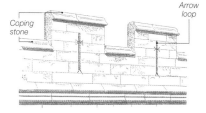

Exterior view

Arrow loop

Coping stone

Interior view

Extension of moulded coping

Arrow loop

Allure

Moulded coping

By the 13th century, the coping stones of the battlements were often being made with a moulded lip projecting over the exterior face. The tactical purpose of this was to prevent arrows glancing off the tops of the parapet into the castle. Sometimes the sides of the merlons were also treated in this way.

Crenellations

The crenellated profile of the parapet had an alternating sequence of merlons and crenels, the latter comprising embrasures through which missiles could be fired. Dimensions varied, but the tendency was for early merlons to be considerably wider than the crenels. From c.1200, merlons were pierced by arrow loops.

Covered allures

Where the allure was covered by a roof or vault, the encircling wall could not be crenellated in the normal sense, though a system of alternating openings and screen walls pierced by arrow loops was incorporated into the build.

Battlements

Swallowtail battlements: Italy
The fashion in Italy was for swallowtail battlements. The inner sides of the merlons were arched to give the crenel a curved V-shape. While said to have indicated allegiance to the Ghibellines (a political faction), their significance is not entirely clear.

Although the general principle of battlements was universal, not all crenellations follow the same pattern. The proportional widths of merlons and crenels vary, and in the later Middle Ages in particular, regional types evolved. Generally, these regional traditions owe little to defensive improvements and more to aesthetic or symbolic considerations. From the 13th century onwards, in addition to their military function, battlements acted as decorative crestings, designed to enhance the ornamental effect of the castle, a role that only increased as the Middle Ages progressed.

Mudéjar battlements: Spain

In Spain, where Islamic building traditions had a considerable influence, a Mudéjar style of merlons developed. These have distinctive pyramidal coping, or caps. They were also influenced by the pitched copings of European battlements, but here were given a three-dimensional quality that is largely decorative.

Stepped battlements: Ireland

In late medieval Ireland, the favoured regional tradition was the stepped or shouldered battlement in which the merlons have a stepped profile. Wider merlons might have two steps instead of one. At the corners of the building, where the merlons form a right angle, finials are formed by upward extensions.

Sculptured battlements: England

In England, from the late 13th century, there was a fashion for battlements to be decorated with sculptures. This phenomenon is associated particularly with the north of England in the 14th century. Sculptures depict warriors, musicians and mythical figures.

Crenel Shutters

Single-shutter grooves
The trunnions of some crenel shutters were accommodated in housings cut into the sides of the merlons. Although the shutters haven't survived, the slots provide evidence of their existence. One end of the pivot bar was set within a hole, and the other within a slot to facilitate removal.

Although the merlons provided some protection for the defenders on the allure, the lack of a continuous screen was a significant weakness in the defensive attributes of the parapet. The measure adopted to remedy this defect was to fit the crenels with shutters. Crenel shutters were made of wood, and held in position by iron fittings that allowed them to pivot on a horizontal plane. This meant they could be opened at will for observation or for discharging projectiles.

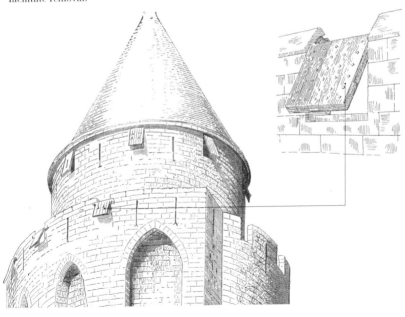

The double shutter

In enclosed allures, the crenels might be fitted with double shutters capable of being operated independently. The enclosed nature of the crenels made fitting and removal more difficult, so it may be that double shutters were intended to facilitate this process.

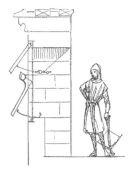

Double shutter section

While the practicalities of assembly and maintenance may have played their part in their design, double shutters also had the advantage of being able to perform separate functions. The upper shutter could be propped open to increase ventilation and light without compromising security.

Upper shutter fixtures

Upper shutters could be hung on iron pintles fixed at the head of the frame, within the external rebate. Because the pintles are fitted into the front of the frame, the rebate is necessary to allow the shutter to be closed flush with the exterior face of the wall.

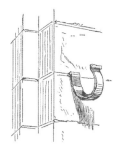

Lower shutter fixtures

A different method was used for fixing the lower shutter. The outer face was fitted with a pivot bar and hung on a pair of iron hinges that were fixed to the face of the wall, one each side of the crenel.

Hoardings

In some castles timber structures known as hoardings might be erected along wallheads. A hoarding comprised an enclosed fighting gallery that was cantilevered out over a wall's exterior face in order to provide an advanced line of defence and to control the area directly in front of the walls. Only one example of a medieval hoarding survives, but information regarding their nature can be found in both contemporary illustrations and from surviving masonry features that accommodated them.

Château de Laval
Generally, medieval hoardings are no longer extant, but a rare survival at the Château de Laval, in northern France, suggests that hoardings may have been intended as permanent structures.

Hoarding beam slots

A common clue to the former existence of
hoarding is one or two rows of beam slots
close to the wallhead. The main beams were
threaded through the wall and the hoarding
constructed on both sides so that there were
two parallel, but interconnected, galleries.

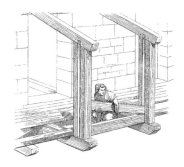

Hoarding construction

The main cantilevered beam, the base
on which the superstructure was built,
extended to either side of the wall. The
crenels of the stone building provided access
to the external gallery, with the platform
erected at the level of the crenel sills.

The hoarding in use

The external gallery of a hoarding was
provided with arrow loops, and missiles
could be dropped through holes in the floor,
which overlooked the base of the walls.
The internal gallery facilitated the rapid
deployment of men and ammunition.

Corbelled supports

In some castles, rather than incorporating
beam slots, the masons provided for
hoardings by building corbelled supports.
It was a first stage in the development
of the stone-corbelled machicolations that
superseded timber hoardings.

Slot Machicolations

One of the advantages of hoardings was that they gave control over the base of the curtain wall. They could therefore be used to hamper attacks on the fabric of the castle and infiltration to it by escalade. The disadvantage of hoardings was that they were made of timber, and were therefore vulnerable both to stone-throwing engines and to fire. A solution was to create a wallhead defensive system that replicated the functions of hoardings in stone, which was stronger and fire-resistant. The slot machicolation was the earliest attempt at creating such a system.

Château Gaillard
One of the first examples of the slot machicolation in Western Europe was on the donjon of Château Gaillard, in Normandy, France. Built in 1196–98, the parapet was supported on a series of wedge-shaped buttresses linked by pointed arches, and the machicolation slots are set over the recesses between the buttresses.

Krak des Chevaliers

A more complete example of slot machicolation, which probably predates that at Château Gaillard, is to be found on the 12th-century north-east tower of the inner enceinte at Krak des Chevaliers, in Syria. The device is very obviously protecting the base of its exposed side.

North-east tower

Batters

Machicolation slots

Krak des Chevaliers (plan)

The plan of the north-east tower shows that the three machicolation slots, which were each roughly 3.5-m (11½-ft) long, could be used to discharge very considerable missiles of devastating force. The batter at the tower would have rendered them all the more dangerous due to the ricochet action it facilitated.

The Popes' Palace

The slot machicolation was largely superseded during the later medieval period, but was used extensively in at least one major fortified residence during the 14th century. This was The Popes' Palace at Avignon, in the south of France, where the combination of battered plinth and machicolation supporting buttresses results in a powerful fortification.

Corbelled Machicolations

WALLHEAD DEFENCE

Box machicolations

Box machicolation, an early type of corbelled machicolation, was developed in the Middle East. During the first half of the 13th century, it was deployed along the outer curtain of Krak des Chevaliers, in Syria, forming a series of corbelled and stone-roofed projections accessible from a vaulted gallery behind the curtain wall.

An alternative to the slot machicolation was the corbelled machicolation, which developed during the 13th century. In this system, a line of corbels supported an oversailing parapet and the machicolation openings were situated between the corbels. Corbelled machicolations evolved from timber hoardings, the corbels replacing the horizontal timber beams that supported the superstructure of a hoarding. The advantage over slot machicolations was that they did not require such a substantial substructure, but a disadvantage was that the openings were smaller and therefore less versatile.

Tiered corbels
From the 14th century, extravagant machicolations on multiple tiers of corbels became an essential part of the wallhead panoply of defence in France, although there was less enthusiasm in England. However, while the prime purpose was defensive, there is no doubt that there was also an ornamental aspect to the form.

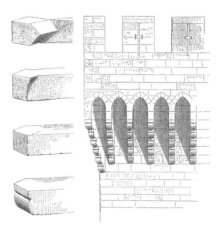

Design and construction
Arched machicolations on corbels at the corner of a building required a high degree of precision. The craftsmen behind the 14th-century machicolations of The Popes' Palace at Avignon, in the south of France, had to contend with numerous planes, including the two faces of the parapet, the obliquely angled sides of the corbels and the curve of the arch.

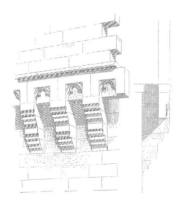

Aesthetics
Late medieval machicolations could be both practical and decorative, as this early-15th-century example at Tarascon Castle, in the south of France, shows. The corbels are alternately hollowed and roll-moulded in order to create contrasts of light and shade, and blind trefoil-arched lintels emphasise the intervening openings.

Tiered Wallhead Defence

Hoarding section: Château de Coucy

This cross-section illustrates the reconstructed hoarding of the Coucy donjon, in Picardy, France. There are two levels of defence, the first conducted from a platform behind the wall, using arrow loops in the masonry beneath the level of the hoard; and the second from the hoard itself, outside the wall.

The replacement of timber hoardings with stone machicolations resulted in stronger and more permanent structures. However, owing to the heavier and less flexible nature of stone, it wasn't possible to produce faithful replications of the timber structures in their entirety. Specifically, whereas timber hoardings facilitated the deployment of more than one tier of wallhead defence, such arrangements could not be reproduced in stone. During the 14th century, castle builders, particularly in France, devised alternative systems that attained the same end and resulted in more spectacular architectural character.

The two-tier hoarding

Documentary references suggest the existence of two-storey hoardings, and this is not at all improbable. Timber is relatively light and flexible in construction. In combination with masonry arrow loops, it should have been possible to achieve three tiers of defence.

Masonry wallhead: Château de Pierrefonds

It was impractical to replicate tiered defence systems in stone. However, by the late 14th century, castle builders had devised a masonry scheme that incorporated the general principle. At Château de Pierrefonds, near Paris, for example, there are three tiers of crenels and arrow loops.

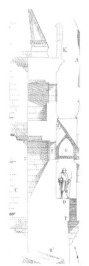

Masonry wallhead section: Château de Pierrefonds

The three tiers at Pierrefonds are, firstly, the machicolated gallery, with its front wall carried on corbels and its lean-to roof against the rear wall. Behind and above the gallery is a storey pierced by crenels, and above that is the crenellated parapet of the external allure.

Masonry wallhead construction: Château de Pierrefonds

At the level of the machicolated gallery, the exterior wall narrows so that the first allure is on a ledge of the wall. The wall is carried up behind the gallery to create another storey that, like the gallery, is pierced by crenels and arrow loops. The crenellated parapet forms another level of defence.

Introduction

The main gateway was nearly always associated with a tower, being either contained within one, or flanked by one or two towers. The entrance and its accompanying tower(s) comprised the gatehouse. Early gatehouses were rectangular and usually with a single tower, a form probably determined by timber prototypes. In several 11th-century stone gatehouses, the gateway opens into an entrance hall rather than a passage. Arrangements such as this may also echo timber structures. In later gatehouses, passages are the norm.

The gate passage
Because the gate was vulnerable to attack by fire, the gate passage was usually stone-vaulted. A barrel vault was a functional and cost-effective method of achieving this; better-quality barrel vaulting was built on a framework of ribs. Occasionally, a more decorative form of rib vault was used to create an impressive display.

Reconstruction

Few 11th- or early-12th-century gatehouses have survived in their original state. The first floor of the gatehouse of Prudhoe Castle, in Northumberland, was rebuilt in the 13th century, and an extra storey was added in the 14th century, but the early-12th-century lower storey was retained.

A two-way gatehouse: Margat Castle

The entrance to Margat Castle, in Syria, is rather unusual. Though outwardly conventional, it is pierced on both sides rather than containing a straightforward through passage. One gate gives access to the castle and the other leads to the fortified town with which it is associated.

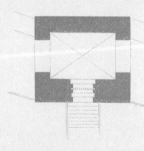

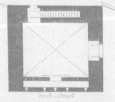

Ground-floor: Margat Castle (plan)

The gate passage, which was protected by a box machicolation and a portcullis, gave access to a cross-vaulted entrance hall. The openings in the side walls led to the castle (right) and the town (left).

First-floor: Margat Castle (plan)

Neither the first floor or battlements communicated with the ground floor. The portcullis was controlled from the vaulted first-floor, and a mural gallery along the entrance front gave access to the box machicolation. A mural staircase led from the entrance lobby to the battlements.

Twin-Towered Gateways

**Polygonal towers:
Warkworth Castle**
Semi-polygonal towers
appeared at Warkworth,
in Northumberland,
c.1200. The multiple
facets of the towers
allowed a broad field
of fire from the arrow
loops. The entrance was
protected by a portcullis
and murder holes in
the vault of the gate
passage. Towards the
end of the 14th century,
the gatehouse was
raised in height.

From the late 12th century it became a common
practice for gateways to be flanked by a pair of towers.
Twin towers projecting in front of the gateway made
it possible to conduct a more effective defence of this
vulnerable position. Subsequently, twin towers were
linked by a room that extended over the gate passage,
and from which the portcullis and drawbridge
mechanisms were operated. The earliest twin gateway
towers were rectangular in plan but the turn of the
12th and 13th centuries witnessed more experimentation
in their design.

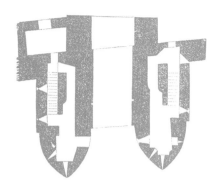

Beaked towers: Porte Saint-Jean

Another unusual plan of the late 12th and early 13th centuries was the beaked tower, a form that echoed the beaked donjons of the period. A gatehouse with flanking towers of this type was built at Porte Saint-Jean, in the Loire Valley, France, its towers projecting boldly beyond the walls.

Appended towers: Laon Gate

A common plan of the 13th century was to append the flanking drum towers to the corners of a rectangular block, which then formed the nucleus of the gatehouse, as shown in this plan of the Laon Gate of Coucy-le-Châteu, in Picardy, France. The plan gave the gatehouse capacity to be used as a residence.

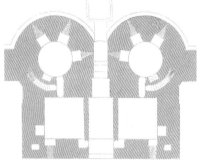

Drum gate: Rockingham Castle

From the early 13th century onwards, the most popular form of flanking tower was the drum tower. This could be of circular or D-shaped plan so that the entrance was recessed within a double-bowed front. At Rockingham Castle, in Northamptonshire, the gatehouse was modernised in the late 13th century by the addition of twin D-shaped towers.

The Great Gatehouse

During the 13th century, when the emphasis was on the development of the enceinte, and when, in some cases, the great tower was eschewed altogether, a type of gatehouse that had some of the qualities of a great tower developed. These so-called gatehouse keeps evolved from the twin-towered gatehouse, to which was added a rectangular residential block containing substantial domestic accommodation. At the same time, the defensive capability of the gatehouse was retained. These elements coalesced into a unified structure that became an established and popular architectural type during the late 13th century.

Laon Gate: Coucy-le-Château

An early example of the type is the Laon Gate, one of the entrances to the walled town of Coucy-le-Chateau, in Picardy, France. It was built sometime between 1215 and 1242. Defended by a drawbridge, a portcullis, tiers of arrow loops and hoardings over the entrance and around the towers, it contained a first-floor hall in the block to the rear.

Tonbridge Castle

One of the earliest gatehouse keeps in England, at Tonbridge Castle in Kent, dates from the 1250s. It had a hall on the second floor and private chambers on the first floor. The rear elevation displays the more domestic aspect of the building, contrasting with the closely set drum towers of the more martial front elevation.

Caernarfon Castle

Several gatehouse keeps were built on the model of Tonbridge during Edward I's 13th-century conquest of Wales. Something different was planned (though never completed) for the King's Gate at Caernarfon Castle, North Wales: the gatehouse was intended to extend right across the castle to divide it into two baileys.

Denbigh Castle (plan)

Some aspects of the intended form of the King's Gate at Caernarfon might be seen in the main entrance to Denbigh Castle, also in Wales, begun in 1282 with royal assistance.

The Denbigh gatehouse, which probably dates from the 1290s, has a roughly triangular plan with an octagonal tower at each angle and a central octagonal entrance hall.

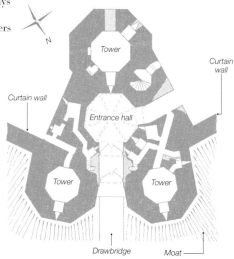

Gatehouses

The 13th century had been dominated by the twin-drum-towered gatehouse, a type that culminated in the gatehouse keep. Although the monumental character of the gatehouse keep remained a popular model into the late medieval period, the trend in the 14th century was away from the overtly martial air that had characterised many 13th-century buildings, and towards greater elegance. The twin-towered gatehouse design was the most prevalent manifestation of this new style, but other types were also built.

Villeneuve-lés-Avignon
The legacy of the gatehouse keep is to be seen in gatehouses like that of the late-14th-century castle at Villeneuve-lés-Avignon, in the south of France. The continuous line of the parapet across the front, on heavy machicolations, is in accord with contemporary French practice at the Bastille and Tarascon.

Maxstoke Castle

A vogue for gatehouses with twin polygonal flanking towers prevailed in mid-14th-century England. Maxstoke Castle, in Warwickshire, has serious defensive qualities, but aesthetics were also an important factor in the design. The gatehouse embodies both aspects, but the central position and great height suggest that architectural impact was uppermost.

Puerta de Serranos

The Puerta de Serranos, in Valencia, Spain, is a gateway of similar date to Maxstoke Castle – c.1349. This, too, has polygonal towers, but above the gate is a delicate, blind-traceried arcade, and around the upper storey, a corbelled gallery (restored). The gatehouse is open-backed.

Brougham Castle

The single-towered rectangular gatehouse is an early type, but several later medieval examples are known. The 14th-century gatehouse at Brougham Castle, in Cumbria, is recognisably of its date due to its decorative window tracery, corbelled machicolation and diagonally placed corner turrets.

Later Gatehouses

The 15th century brought no particular innovations in gatehouse design. The adoption of the integrated plan for many new castles of the late medieval period meant that new gatehouses became less of a separate entity and, in a few cases, the entrance became little more than a vaulted passageway through one of the accommodation ranges. In other instances the visual impact of the great gatehouse was too great to be ignored and the gatehouse front was retained in the form of a monumental centrepiece.

Herstmonceux Castle
Built c.1441, the gatehouse of Herstmonceux Castle, in Sussex, has a firmly martial appearance. It employs several tiers of cruciform arrow loops, a lower tier of gun loops, a machicolated parapet carried across the space between the twin towers, murder holes above the entrance arch and slots for the drawbridge beams. However, there is also an emphasis on formality and display.

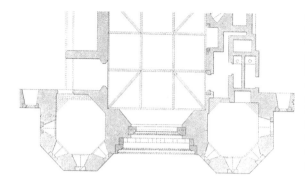

Gateway: Herstmonceux Castle (plan)

The Herstmonceux gateway gave access to what might be called an entrance hall rather than a passage, covered with a ribbed vault. Originally, there was no access from here to the adjacent ranges but there was a porter's lodge in one of the flanking towers.

Raglan Castle

Dating from the 1460s, the gatehouse of Raglan Castle, in Wales, is flanked by a pair of semi-hexagonal towers, whose extravagant arched machiolations suggest French influence. All the windows have a very domestic appearance and the only arrow loops are in the merlons, although there is a gun loop covering the approach to the gate.

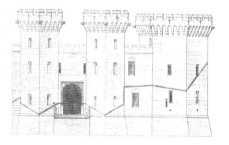

Belmonte Castle

In castles of concentric design, in which there is an outer curtain with its own entrance, the outer gatehouse is invariably smaller than the principal gatehouse to the inner bailey. Dating from c.1456, the outer gatehouse to Belmonte Castle, in central Spain, is comparatively low, with a broad front flanked by two round towers.

Murder Holes

The so-called 'murder hole' is a type of machicolation largely confined to gateways. It consists of an opening, often one of a group of similar features, in the vault or elevation of a gate passage that could be used by the occupants on the floor above. In the past they have been explained as a means by which the defenders of a castle could harry an enemy with missiles in the event of them gaining unauthorised access to the gate passage, but alternative interpretations, including their use as a supply hatch, are equally, if not more valid.

The service hatch
One of these alternative interpretations applies to a large murder hole over the Narbonne Gate at Carcassonne. The hatch pierces not only the vault of the gate passage, but also that of the first-floor room. It was probably designed for hauling goods to the upper storeys of the gatehouse.

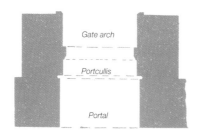

Ground floor: Caerphilly Castle (plan)

An interesting sequence survives at the main east gate of Caerphilly Castle, a building designed for independent defence. At ground level the inner end of the gate passage progresses through an open portal, then a portcullis and then the gate.

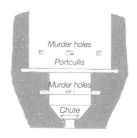

First-floor: Caerphilly Castle (plan)

Above the entrance are two lines of murder holes. The first line lies over the portal and the second between the portcullis and the gate. An additional hole, in the form of an oblique chute, opens out on the elevation above the entrance.

Elevation: Caerphilly Castle

The slot in the masonry above the gateway is a water chute, fed by a mural channel from first-floor level. Such devices were designed to dowse any fire that might be raised against the gate by allowing water to be poured onto it.

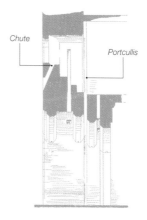

Section: Caerphilly Castle

The water chute was supplied from the first-floor window embrasure, as was the first line of murder holes, the two outer ones forming channels down the side walls. The second line of murder holes was used from the adjacent room.

Posterns

The water gate

In castles situated close to the sea or a river estuary, it would be normal to have a postern giving direct access to the water. The c.1295 water gate at Beaumaris Castle, on the Isle of Anglesey in Wales, was associated with a dock in front of the castle walls.

In addition to the main gateway, there was usually at least one other, smaller entrance to a castle – the postern gate. Some posterns, known as sally posts, are believed to be related to an aggressive defence policy. They provided a means by which the inmates of the castle might launch unobtrusive sorties against a besieging force. Others, however, were clearly intended as service entrances, connected with provisioning and other domestic necessities. From its disposition and character, it is often possible to discern the specific purpose of a particular gateway.

Warkworth Castle
A postern at Warkworth Castle, in Northumberland, opens to the top of a steep bank extending down to the River Coquet. The situation of the postern next to the castle kitchen suggests that one function was to accept the delivery of provisions transported by water.

Elevated postern: Château de Pierrefonds
Where there was a disparity between the height of the courtyard and the ground level, a postern might be in a considerably elevated position. At Pierrefonds, in Picardy, France, the main postern is c.10 m (33 ft) above ground level. It must have had a means of approach that is no longer evident.

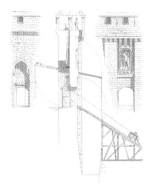

Inclined plane: Château de Pierrefonds
Goods were raised on an inclined plane attached to the postern by a drawbridge. A windlass situated on the allure above the postern was used to haul items up the inclined plane by rope.

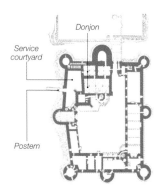

Donjon

Service courtyard

Postern

Service yard: Château de Pierrefonds (plan)
The postern at Pierrefonds was situated to give access to a service courtyard in the shadow of the donjon. This provided a good-sized holding area that was close to the storage areas in the donjon.

Drawbridge

Most castles were defended by a ditch or moat so that, in order to maintain access to the entrance, it was necessary to provide a bridge. However, to avoid compromising the defence, it had to be a retractable bridge. The solution was the drawbridge, a device that was raised by some form of mechanism, which both prevented unauthorised access and formed an additional defensive barrier in front of the gate. Although no medieval drawbridges survive, the type of mechanism involved can often be discerned from architectural remains.

Lifting bridge
In one of the simplest forms of mechanised drawbridge, the inner end of the bridge was hinged on the threshold of the gate and the outer end was attached, by chains, to a windlass within the gatehouse. As the windlass was turned, the drawbridge was raised or lowered.

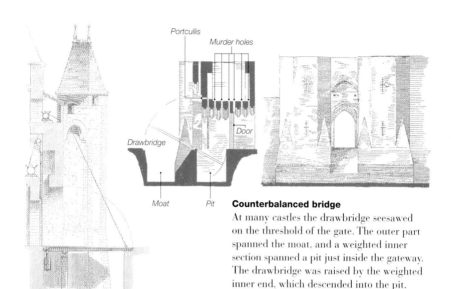

Portcullis Murder holes

Drawbridge

Door

Moat Pit

Counterbalanced bridge
At many castles the drawbridge seesawed
on the threshold of the gate. The outer part
spanned the moat, and a weighted inner
section spanned a pit just inside the gateway.
The drawbridge was raised by the weighted
inner end, which descended into the pit,
while the outer end blocked the entrance.

Lifting bridge section
This section shows the chains
extending from the outer end of
the bridge to the windlass above
the gate. To facilitate raising the
bridge its inner end is weighted.

Counterbalanced beams
A new type of drawbridge came
into use c.1300. In this, a pair
of long beams was pivoted above
and at either side of the gateway.
The beams were attached to the
bridge by chains and the inner
ends were weighted to act as a
counterbalance, by which method
the bridge was raised. When
vertical, the beams fitted into
specially designed slots.

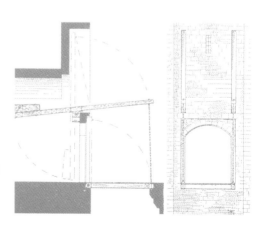

Portcullis

Main gateways, posterns and other significant external entrances were often protected by a portcullis. Constructed of wood, and in the form of a grill, the portcullis was a vertical gate suspended above the entrance and lowered into position when required. The portcullis was operated from above by winding machinery and was guided by grooves cut into the stonework on either side of the entrance. The feet of the timber verticals were pointed and clad in iron. Portcullises were used by the Romans, and had been introduced into castles by the early 12th century.

External portcullis
Most portcullises could be withdrawn into the building, leaving only the feet protruding. Some, however, were exposed to view within a recess at the front of the gatehouse, even when in the raised position. Whether this arrangement was believed to have some practical advantage is uncertain.

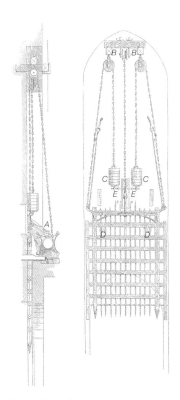

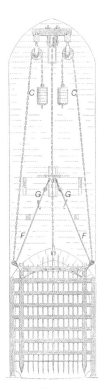

Narbonne Gate: Carcassonne

The portcullis is raised and lowered
by a chain, one end of which is attached
to a pulley and the other to a windlass (A).
Two other chains extend from the ends of
the portcullis over two further pulleys (B),
and terminate in counterweights (C).
The portcullis is held in the raised position
by two retractable horizontal beams (D)
that protrude from the wall behind it, and
the counterweights are locked in position
by anchoring them to a metal rod secured
by hooks (E).

To lower the portcullis, the two supporting
beams (D) and the metal rod (E) anchoring
the counterweights (C) are removed. The
weight of the portcullis allows a rapid
descent. A pair of iron bars (F) attached
to the top of the portcullis are locked into
position by iron pins (G) protruding from
the wall. When they are thus locked, the
portcullis cannot be raised.

Gates

Drawbridges and portcullises gave additional protection to an entrance, but were supplementary to, rather than substitutes for, a conventional gate. The gates were usually made of wood, hinged at the sides, and double-leaved, and there was often one at each end of the entrance passage. However, numerous designs of castle gate existed, and although the gates themselves do not normally survive, their nature, including how they were hung, locked and operated, can often be reconstructed from surviving stone and metal housings.

Top-hung gates
The operation of some gates was inspired by drawbridge mechanisms. In the horizontally hung gate, which in this case was controlled by a windlass situated above the gate passage, the weight of the gate allowed it to be lowered rapidly.

Centre-hung gates

Drawbridge technology is also evident in another type of horizontally hung gate, which was pivoted at its centre, at the head of the gateway. Here too, gravity played its part in allowing a rapid descent.

The drawbar

When not in use, a drawbar was lodged within a long socket on one side of the door embrasure. When gates needed securing, it could be rapidly withdrawn, pulled across the door, and secured in a notch on the opposite side of the embrasure.

The pivoted bar

In this type, the gates are hinged in stone housings and a bar is fixed to one of the leaves so that it can be pivoted to secure the gates. When closed, the ends of the bar slot into grooves cut into the adjacent walls.

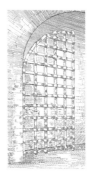

The yett

Iron gates were also used at the entrances to medieval castles. In northern England and Scotland, where they are known as 'yetts', they were popular during the 14th and 15th centuries.

Introduction

In addition to being endowed with various protective devices, many gatehouses were also given a barbican. A barbican was a fortified outwork through which the visitor to a castle had to pass before reaching the gate, and its purpose was to attach an additional level of control over access to the castle, for defensive or policing purposes. In military terms, it lessened the chance of a surprise attack on the gatehouse, and it also had the ability to confine an attacker to a relatively small and exposed area, which was commanded by the gatehouse.

Château Comtal

Some barbicans were of elaborate construction. An extreme example is the elongated and fortified approach to the Château Comtal of Carcassonne, in south-west France. A walled passageway climbed from a circular enclosure at the foot of the hill, making a 90-degree turn before connecting with the citadel.

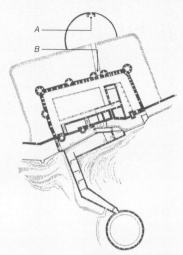

Lesser barbican: Château Comtal (plan)

Château Comtal had two barbicans; one for each of its two main gates. The one towards the walled town was a less elaborate affair, comprising a semi-circular enclosure (A) with a passageway leading from it to the gateway (B). It was still a significant aspect of the fortifications, and it is clear that access to the castle from both directions was rigorously controlled.

The barbican passage

For topographical reasons, most barbicans were simpler and more compact than those at Carcassonne. Nevertheless, they were serious fortifications designed to protect the gatehouse, and from which the approach might be monitored, and often provided with their own gates and drawbridges.

Prudhoe Castle (plan)

In a moated castle, the barbican might be incorporated into a fortified bridge. At Prudhoe Castle, in Northumberland, the barbican originally extended from the gatehouse to the lip of the moat. An outwork was later built on the outer side of the moat and the two structures were linked by a bridge to create an elongated barbican.

Courtyard Barbicans

One of the two principal types of barbican was the courtyard barbican. This was an enclosure in front of the gate defined by a wall or palisade. It was usually, but not always, outside the main castle ditch and connected to the gatehouse by a bridge. The courtyard barbican had its own curtain and gateway, and sometimes had its own ditch. While there was no set pattern to the design, occasionally a common concept was replicated at more than one castle site, perhaps indicating the work of one engineer.

Saint-Lazare Gate

The military thinking behind courtyard barbicans is clear in this reconstruction of the 14th-century Saint-Lazare Gate at Avignon, in the south of France. Any assault on the gateway itself was untenable without taking the barbican. However, as the barbican is overlooked by the gatehouse, it could not be held.

Saint-Lazare Gate (plan)

The plan reinforces the military significance of the barbican. Because the entrance is in the side wall, the barbican breaks up the line of approach to the gatehouse and thereby impedes the impetus of an assault. In contrast with the three outer walls, the side towards the gatehouse is open, giving the defenders in the gatehouse a clear view of the enclosure.

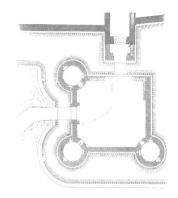

The timber barbican

The courtyard barbican may often have been made of timber, a medium that seldom survives in castle defences. It may once have been more common. The timber barbican shown in this copy of a medieval illustration had its own twin-towered gatehouse and pivoted gate, and was evidently intended to play an important defensive role.

Conwy Castle (plan)

The nature of the site played its part in determining the character of the barbican. Conwy Castle, in Wales, crowns a long, narrow, rocky prominence. Its two barbicans occupy either end of the site. Both gateways are very simple, and the barbicans make up for the lack of a gatehouse.

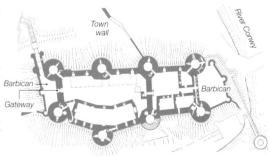

Passageway Barbicans

Alnwick Castle

The passageway barbican in front of the main gateway to Alnwick Castle, in Northumberland, is very well preserved. A mid-14th century example, the recessed entrance is set between a pair of square turrets and gives access to a very tightly regulated approach.

The passageway barbican, an alternative to the courtyard barbican, is the type most in evidence today. Attached to the front of the gatehouse, forming an extension to the gate passage, and rising high enough to cover the gateway, it was a more constricted feature. The entrance to a passageway barbican was sometimes protected by a gate, sometimes by a portcullis and sometimes by both. The crenellated parapet usually protected an allure, which might be reached from inside the gatehouse or from within the barbican itself.

The allure

The allure at Alnwick was not accessible from inside the barbican, only from the gatehouse to which it was attached. It was protected by double battlements, which gave the defenders a military advantage and greater control of the passage, in which traffic could be inspected before being granted entry to the castle.

Vaulted entrance

Alnwick's vaulted entrance opened to a tall, narrow, unroofed passage commanded for its entire length from the parapet. A ditch ran from one side of the barbican to the other and was crossed by a pivoted drawbridge that could be drawn up in front of the gateway.

The allure

The allure extended around all three sides so that the well of the barbican was commanded completely from this level. It also gave access to the roof over the entrance passage at the front of the barbican, and to a pair of staircases that ascended to the parapets of the turrets flanking the entrance.

Introduction

Berkeley Castle

At Berkeley Castle, in Gloucestershire, the great hall on the right is identifiable from its tall transomed windows, the height of which denotes a single-storey building. The porch at the left-hand end of the hall indicates the position of the entrance. Typically, the kitchen and service rooms were located on the other side of the hall entrance.

The domestic accommodation in castles was focused on the communal dining room known as the great hall. In close proximity to the great hall were the service rooms in which comestibles were stored and prepared. Chief of these was the kitchen, but they included the pantry, the buttery and other specialist areas. The private accommodation of the lord was also associated with the hall. This could, in larger establishments, form quite an elaborate suite of rooms, known collectively as a chamber block.

The great hall

The importance of the hall as the focus of the residential apartments is emphasised in this medieval manuscript illustration of a castle. The hall, with its large, traceried windows and pitched roof, looms above the curtain wall to dominate the interior.

Berkeley Castle (plan)

Entrance to the great hall was nearly always at the 'lower' end of one or both of the side walls. Within the hall, there was more than one door in the 'lower' end wall leading to the kitchen and services. The 'upper' end wall usually held access to the lord's private apartments, often on an upper storey.

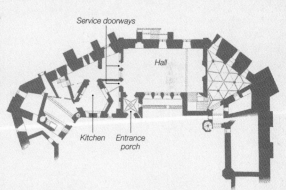

Service doorways

Hall

Kitchen *Entrance porch*

The high table

The dais, at the 'upper' end of the hall, was occupied by the high table, where the lord and his guests sat on the occasions that he dined with the general company. The dais was usually a wooden structure, often covered by a canopy, decorated with hangings and sometimes provided with its own fireplace.

Early Great Halls

The tripartite nature of the aisled form can be appreciated fully in the great hall of Oakham Castle, in Rutland. The building, c.1180–90, has a high central 'nave' with its own roof, and two low side aisles with individual lean-to roofs. Doorways in the gable end suggest that the hall was formerly linked to subsidiary buildings.

Early great halls were often of aisled construction so that, like a church, arcades divided the interior into a central 'nave' and side aisles – sometimes there was only a single aisle. The purpose of the division was that it allowed a building of greater width than would have been technically possible if it had to be roofed in a single span. As it was, the presence of arcades allowed the 'nave' to be roofed independently of the aisles. For this reason the larger great halls of the 12th century tended to be of aisled construction.

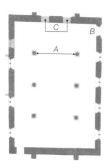

Oakham Castle (plan)

Cylindrical columns (A) supported the arcades that divided the hall. The entrance (B) was at the east end of the south wall into the eastern bay. From this 'lower' end there was access to the service rooms (C).

Interior: Oakham Castle

Although the 12th-century roof has been replaced, the supportive function of the arcades is clear. The original structure was probably a simple collar-rafter roof with the rafter ends held by a timber wall plate running to the top of each arcade.

A great hall within a keep (plan)

Great halls are also to be encountered within keeps, as at Castle Hedingham, Essex, where the hall is located on the uppermost storey of the tower built in the 1140s by Aubrey de Vere, Earl of Oxford.

Interior: Hedingham Castle

Although the spatial characteristics of the great hall were constrained by the confines of the keep, a grand effect is produced by extending the room through two storeys and by framing the upper end with an enormous arch.

Mid-Medieval Great Halls

From the 13th century, attempts were made to roof great halls without recourse to aisles. Advances in carpentry resulted in several technical solutions being developed during the 13th and 14th centuries. The result was a more cohesive external appearance, and a more commodious interior with greater possibilities for spectacle and display (always an important aspect of great halls). It is probable, too, that the technological virtuosity of the carpentry itself was an object of admiration. One provincial fortified manor house in which this trend can be observed is Stokesay Castle, in Shropshire.

Stokesay Castle

The technology used to create a single-span roof over the great hall of Stokesay Castle was based on cruck construction, a form local to Shropshire. This represents a deliberate move away from aisled construction: the structure of the roof is related to a raised aisle truss set against the end wall.

Exterior: Stokesay Castle

The low level of the eaves found in aisled halls sometimes survived even when the aisles had been dispensed with. A 13th-century development to provide greater illumination to buildings of this type was the introduction of gables over the main windows to allow taller windows.

Stokesay Castle (plan)

The plan of the residential block at Stokesay shows how significant the hall was in the wider scheme. It occupies the central and greater part of the main range. The two end blocks contained storage areas and, above them, residential accommodation.

Hall

Cellar

Acton Burnell Castle

Most great halls have dependent structures attached to them, but at Acton Burnell Castle, in Shropshire, the first-floor hall (recognisable from its large windows) was entirely subsumed within the greater building. This degree of integration was to become common in some of the compact castles of the later Middle Ages.

Late Medieval Great Halls

Kenilworth Castle
A number of late
medieval castle halls
were built at first-floor
level. At Kenilworth
Castle, in Warwickshire,
the late-14th-century
hall was built on an
undercroft. The five
bays of the first-floor
hall are recognisable
from the very tall
windows (interrupted
by the fireplace and
chimney). To the right
are the plain service
rooms, and to the left
the private apartments
with their ornate
windows.

The origins of the medieval great hall lay in the need
to accommodate a great household. This included not
only the owner's family, but also the many servants
necessary for the efficient running of a large house and
estate, as well as the fluctuating population of visitors
that was drawn to the dwelling of an important man.
The organisation that communal living demanded
resulted in a formalising of the space, so that there was
an element of ritual involved in the use of the great
hall. This formality increased during the late medieval
period, as more complex private accommodation
developed and standards of comfort improved.
Nevertheless, the great hall remained at the heart
of the lordly household, and maintained its position as
a centre of entertainment, ceremony and display.

Elevation: Kenilworth Castle (above)

Unusually for the period, the Kenilworth divisions are reflected in a formal fashion on the exterior elevation, where the normally inward-looking accommodation was given a symmetrical front. The rooms flanking the hall were partly accommodated within square bays or turrets that stand proud of the hall.

Yanwath Hall

Smaller halls, like the largely 15th-century Yanwath Hall in Cumbria, were considerably less well appointed than their richer counterparts, but still have a sense of grandeur due to their open roofs. There were fewer technical difficulties in roofing a narrow hall, the solution at Yanwath being to stiffen the rafters and collars with arch braces.

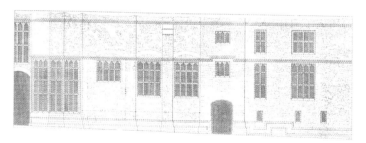

Exterior delineation

The position of a great hall within a greater complex was usually obvious from the exterior. The limits of the great hall of Raglan Castle, in Wales, are defined here by the storied porch to the right and the great bay window to the left, which lit the dais and high table.

Kitchen & Service Rooms

Raby Castle

The kitchen was sometimes in a tower of its own, or at least the principal room within the 'kitchen tower', usually rising through two storeys. The 14th-century kitchen tower of Raby Castle, in Durham, contained a vaulted undercroft, with the kitchen above rising to a vault immediately below the roof.

Adequate food storage and preparation areas were essential to the well-being of a castle's inhabitants, and often formed a significant group of buildings. At the heart of this complex was the kitchen, often a generously proportioned and imposing room, in which large numbers of servants were able to work. Related rooms included the pantry, buttery, larder, pastry, kitchen, scullery and wine cellar. The kitchen and its associated rooms were usually situated within the vicinity of the great hall, conventionally, at its 'lower' end. Some of the more complex households of the later medieval period had more than one kitchen.

Kitchen tower

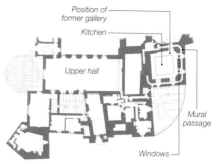

Ground-floor: Raby Castle (plan)

The kitchen tower of Raby Castle, which dates from c.1350, is roughly 14-m (46-ft) square. It was built at the lower end of the hall to serve both ground- and first-floor halls.

Kitchen gallery: Raby Castle (plan)

The windows of the kitchen were at a high level and linked by a mural passage. Stepped sills descended to the kitchen and probably led to a wooden gallery ranged around the tower – possibly storage space or accommodation for the staff.

The kitchen fireplace

The principal feature of a medieval kitchen was its great fireplace. Kitchen fireplaces can usually be readily distinguished from their domestic counterparts by their greater size and number (there were often two or more fireplaces in a kitchen).

The ovens

There was always an oven or ovens for baking bread and pastries. Occasionally, an oven was associated with one of the fireplaces of the great kitchen, but more often it was a separate, circular, domed structure with a wide mouth. The interior was heated by a fire, with the embers raked out before the food was put in to cook.

Introduction

Religion played a major role in medieval life, and the chapel was one of the constant elements of the castle. Where it survives, it is usually one of the most distinctive of castle buildings, although it has to be said that a chapel has occasionally been mistaken for a hall. While all castles had at least one chapel, there were often two and sometimes more. The main chapel was frequently a substantial freestanding building. These have occasionally been preserved as a parish church following the demise of the castle they formerly served.

East window and altar
Like other churches, castle chapels were usually orientated towards the liturgical east, and the east wall was often pierced by a large traceried window. Because of this it is sometimes possible to deduce the position of the chapel from the outside. The altar, which would have been placed at the east end, was sometimes built into the fabric.

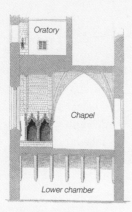

The chapel and oratory

In addition to a principal chapel, there was often a private oratory for the use of the castle's lord. The mid-14th-century chapel and oratory of Beverston Castle, in Gloucestershire, are both associated with the main residential tower, but are on different floors.

The private pew

Many late medieval chapels were built with an integral private pew for the lord, his immediate family and guests. These were in elevated positions at the west end of the chapels. This example at Berkeley Castle, in Gloucestershire, stood in the 14th-century chapel and comprised a main gallery with a more exclusive bay projecting from it.

The piscina

At the east end of the chapel, on the south side, there was nearly always a piscina – an arched niche containing a basin in which the sacred vessels were washed.

The sedilia

The piscina is often accompanied by the sedilia (seats) for the officiating priest(s). A sedile is another arched niche, this time containing a bench.

Gatehouse Chapel

A favoured position for a chapel was in or close to the gatehouse. This association with the entrance is a planning tradition analogous to that of placing the chapel within the forebuilding of a great tower. Gatehouses were one of the focal points of a castle, were neutral areas in the sense that everyone had to use the entrance, and were often readily accessible from the courtyard. It is also possible that a chapel over or next to the entrance was believed to help keep ill-fortune from entering the castle.

Prudhoe Castle
During the 13th century, reconstruction work was done at Prudhoe Castle, in Northumberland. A chapel was created on the first floor of its 12th-century gatehouse, over the entrance. The external clue to this is the weighting of the first floor towards the east (right), where a bay window projects from the building.

The apse: Prudhoe Castle

A sanctuary was created by throwing out an irregular semi-polygonal apse at the east end of the building, pierced by lancet windows and supported on the curtain wall. Effectively, this is an oriel window, a form that only came into its own from the late 14th century onwards.

The sanctuary: Prudhoe Castle

Inside, it is only the east end of the room that betrays its intended function. A broad, pointed arch, symbolising a chancel arch, emphasises the sanctuary, and the identification as a chapel is confirmed by a piscina within the south side of the arch.

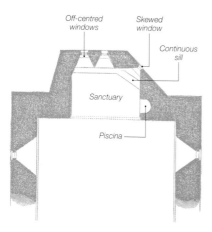

Off-centred windows · Skewed window · Continuous sill · Sanctuary · Piscina

Sanctuary: Prudhoe Castle (plan)

The design oddities of the sanctuary can be discerned from this plan. The feature is irregularly canted, the east windows are off-centre internally and there is a skewed window to the south-east. The reason for these anomalies is not entirely clear, but they seem to be the result of a change of plan. A continuous sill beneath the windows may have served as a repository for sacred vessels and other paraphernalia.

Great Tower Chapel

Where there was a great tower it was often here, in the building most identified with lordship, that the lord's private oratory was to be found. In larger, more complex towers, there might be a fully fledged chapel capable of housing a moderate-sized congregation, which sometimes also catered for the lord's private devotions. The architectural range of the chapel in the great tower, then, is considerable, but most are identifiable through some commonly held conventions.

The White Tower (Tower of London)

One of the earliest great-tower chapels is the 11th-century St John's Chapel in the White Tower, within the Tower of London. The character of the chapel is derived from 11th-century great church architecture. It is an aisled building, with the aisles continuing around the east end in an ambulatory, so that it resembles the eastern arm of a cathedral.

Conisbrough Castle

At Conisbrough Castle, in South Yorkshire, the late-12th-century great-tower chapel was accessible only from the lord's private lodging at third-floor level. The highly decorated interior contrasts with the plain secularity of the other rooms in the keep.

The sanctuary: Warkworth Castle

Some chapels were clearly articulated. In the donjon at Warkworth, in Northumberland, the sanctuary is distinguished by the predella (the raised altar area), and the large east window. The floor above the nave, to the west, formed the private pew of the lord.

The sacristy: Warkworth Castle

Other distinguishing features at Warkworth are the sedile (priest's seat) and piscina. A window embrasure leads to a sacristy – a room for the use of the priest attached to the chapel, where vestments and sacred vessels might be kept. A double squint in the wall enabled the occupant of the sacristy to observe the altar.

College Foundation

St George's Chapel
The greatest of all collegiate castle chapels in England was St George's Chapel, the spiritual home of the Order of the Garter, founded by Edward III in 1348, in Windsor Castle. The chapel was rebuilt by Edward IV in the late 15th century, and, in conjunction with the college buildings, occupies a large part of the lower ward.

During the late Middle Ages, there was a vogue among the nobility for building churches with colleges of priests attached to them within the vicinity of their castles. The prime duty of these priests was to sing masses for the souls of their benefactors. The best known of these 'chantries' is Henry VI's Eton College, near Windsor, but there are numerous others. In a few cases the chantry was based within the castle itself, and centred on the castle chapel. This is so at Bolton Castle, in North Yorkshire, to which a licence for a chantry of six priests was granted in 1393.

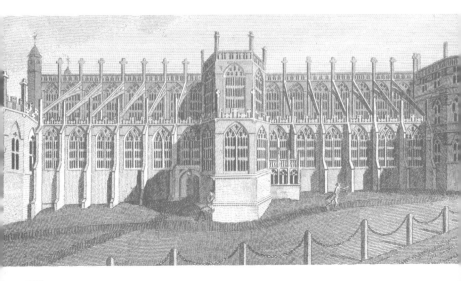

Warkworth Castle (plan)

One of the most ambitious collegiate chapels within the walls of a castle would have been the one at Warkworth Castle, in Northumberland, had it ever been completed. Intended as a cruciform church, it was planned to stretch right across the bailey and to create a small inner courtyard in front of the donjon.

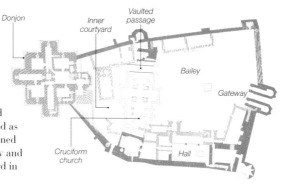

Donjon

Inner courtyard

Vaulted passage

Bailey

Gateway

Cruciform church

Hall

Keep: Warkworth Castle

Although the Warkworth scheme was never entirely fulfilled, the completed base incorporated two vaulted undercrofts, and a broad passage that provided communication between the outer bailey and a small inner courtyard at the foot of the donjon.

Chapel bases: Warkworth Castle

The work did extend to completion of the column bases, which included the four-lobed arcade bases and the more substantial crossing bases designed to take the weight of a central tower. Had the work come to fruition it would have been a significant addition to ecclesiastical architecture.

Introduction

Castles are often associated with imprisonment. As secure buildings, they were appropriate places of confinement and were, on occasion, used to house prisoners. Many prisoners of royal or noble rank were held in castles, either awaiting ransom after capture on the battlefield, pending trial for political crimes, or in the case of deposed monarchs, because they posed a potential threat to the new regime. A castle lord might also find a prison cell useful for suspected criminals, for disciplining his servants or for incarcerating enemies.

The donjon

The great tower was a symbol of lordship, but it might also be associated with oppression. It is instructive that the English word 'dungeon' is derived from the French 'donjon'. There are certainly instances of prisons within donjons, and castle prisons were invariably located in basements, as the word dungeon implies.

Tower of London

In England, the castle most associated with imprisonment is the Tower of London, which was used to house prisoners of royal and noble rank from early in the 12th century. It was a secure place close to the centre of power that could offer accommodation befitting its elite inhabitants.

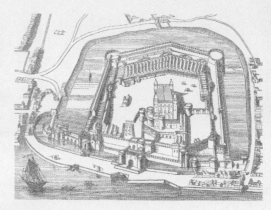

Dürnstein Castle

The castle of Dürnstein, which stands on a rock above the Danube, in Austria, was the castle of Leopold, Duke of Austria. It was here that King Richard I of England was first held after being taken prisoner on his return from the Third Crusade. He was later transferred to Trifels Castle, in south-west Germany.

Pontefract Castle

Destroyed during the English Civil War, Pontefract Castle, in West Yorkshire, was one of the great castles of northern England. By the late 14th century, it was part of the Duchy of Lancaster estate. However, it is notorious as the prison to which Richard II was transferred after his abdication, and the place where he died in mysterious circumstances c.1400.

Prisons

Most castles probably had at least one custom-built prison, and some undoubtedly had several. Those that have been recognised usually occupy a basement room, which gives credence to the popular concept of the castle dungeon as an underground cell devoid of comfort. Rooms that were most obviously cells are those that are entered only by trap in the vault or ceiling. Rooms of this type have sometimes been interpreted as floor safes in which treasure was stored, and the determining factor in interpreting them as prison cells is the provision of a latrine.

Ventilation shaft

Window

Courtyard level

Caesar's Tower

An undoubted prison cell can be found in the basement of the mid-14th-century Caesar's Tower in Warwick Castle, in Warwickshire. This vaulted room, which lies below the level of the courtyard, has a ventilation shaft on one side and a window set high up on the wall on the other. Its only other comfort was a mural latrine.

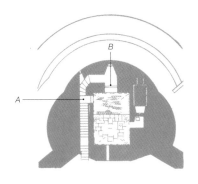

Caesar's Tower (plan)

The staircase descended to a lobby from which the cell was entered (A). However, another mural stair led from the lobby to the embrasure of the window that overlooked the cell (B). Protected by an iron grid, the gaoler would have been able to keep the cell under surveillance without having to enter.

Upper cells: Château de Pierrefonds (plan)

In the Château de Pierrefonds, near Paris, four of the eight wall towers accommodate two-tier prisons in their lower storeys. In each case the upper room is approached from the foot of a spiral staircase (A) via a passage (B) closed by two doors. The room itself is lit by two loops (C) and is provided with a latrine (D).

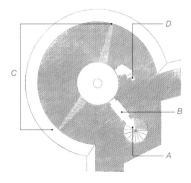

Lower cells: Château de Pierrefonds

In the floor of the upper cell, an opening provided the only access to the lower cell. This was a domed space, without light or ventilation, although it was provided with a latrine. The skeleton of a woman was discovered in the latrine recess of one of these cells during the 19th-century restoration.

Introduction

The porch

The porch served
a practical purpose:
it reduced the draught
from the entrance
and provided an area
in which suppliants
might wait before
being ushered into the
presence of the lord
or his official. It also
had an architectural
function: it emphasised
the castle's principal
domestic building.

The doorway is one of the numerous minor features
that contribute to the overall interpretation of a castle.
Like other architectural details, the doorway was
subject to changing fashion, and the succession of
forms provides useful dating evidence. Differences in
style between contemporary openings within a single
building might also throw light on status and function.
The more pronounced the opening, the more significant
the room to which it gave access, and from the
13th century, the entrance to many a great hall was
accentuated with a porch.

A medieval impression

A measure of the significance that might be attached to the porch is to be found in this manuscript illustration, the emphasis being on the porch rather than on the hall to which it is subordinate.

The architectural porch

The porch might be used to serve as an emphatic architectural introduction to the main domestic apartments. The porch to the great hall of Warkworth Castle, in Northumberland, built c.1480, rises to three storeys and supports a sculptured heraldic array above the entrance.

The embrasure

The thick walls of castles meant that doorways, especially external doorways, were often set within deep recesses, or embrasures. The rear arch (over the embrasure) is usually set at a higher level than the door, and does not necessarily follow the profile of the doorway itself.

Early Medieval Doorways

Doorways with semi-circular arches were used throughout the 11th and 12th centuries and into the 13th century. However, by the late 12th century, new forms were beginning to appear in the more forward-looking buildings as the Gothic style of architecture made its influence felt. Of these new forms, the two-centred, pointed arch was the most widely used for higher-class entrances, for example, in the better domestic apartments, where aesthetics were deemed to be of more importance. Other 13th-century types include the segmental and segmental-pointed arches and the Caernarvon arch.

The semi-circular arch
The most prevalent form of doorway during the 11th and 12th centuries was the semi-circular-arched entrance. This entrance to the great hall of Oakham Castle, in Rutland, is a late example, dating from the end of the 12th century. Its highly decorative character shows that it gives access to a significant room.

The two-centred arch

Doorways with two-centred pointed arches, which were introduced into castles from the late 12th century, were one of the principal types throughout the 13th and 14th centuries, and into the 15th.

The Caernarvon arch

The Caernarvon arch was also popular in castles during the 13th and 14th centuries. It is actually a lintel supported on concave corbels rather than an arch, with a continuous chamfer around the opening.

The segmental-pointed doorway

A type widely used in the 13th and 14th centuries was the segmental pointed doorway. The character of the arch can vary considerably depending on the position of the centres from which the segments are struck. In this example of the 1220s, the outer arch is more acute than the inner arch.

Late Medieval Doorways

Several of the doorway types that had been popular in the 13th century continued into the 14th. Among these was the Caernarvon arch, although by the end of the century it was used infrequently and was confined to lesser positions. The pointed arch was popular throughout the 14th century and was also used through much of the 15th century. Segmental and segmental-pointed arches are also found in 14th-century work. It was probably from the segmental-pointed arch that the four-centred arch developed. This new type was to become standard in the late medieval period.

The semi-circular arch
Most semi-circular-arch doorways date from the 11th and 12th centuries, but the form does occasionally occur in later contexts. This entrance to the fortified manor house of Yanwath Hall, in Cumbria, probably dates from the mid- to late 15th century. The continuous moulding around the opening is a sign of late medieval work.

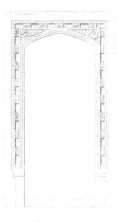

The four-centred arch

Four-centred arches (so called because the design was struck by compasses from four centres) were in use in castles from the late 14th century. This one at Bywell Castle, in Northumberland, dates from c.1420. The arch is made up of two stones and the opening has a continuous hollow moulding.

The four-centred doorway

The four-centred doorway was popular through the 15th and into the 16th century. This refined 1520s example at Thornbury Castle, in Gloucestershire, has carved spandrels and two orders of flanking shafts from which the moulded arch and hood mould spring.

The Tudor arch

Various forms of four-centred arch exist, ranging from the acutely pointed to the almost flat Tudor arch. This Tudor-arch doorway from Thornbury Castle has only a very slight curvature to the inner arcs. It also differs from the shafted doorway in having a continuously moulded surround bordered by rectangular mouldings.

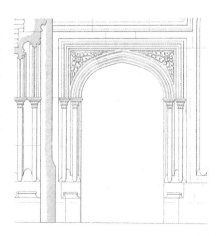

Introduction

In comparison with contemporary ecclesiastical window treatments, castle windows are not always considered a significant aspect of the fabric. While the most exposed windows might be small, mean and infrequent for security reasons, those not in the field of fire could be treated more lavishly and, because castles were homes as well as fortresses, they often were. There was also a hierarchy in design, and this can indicate room function and contribute to our interpretation of how the castle was used.

Window hierarchies
Relationships between rooms can sometimes be read from the external evidence. These two high-quality windows, of similar character, denote two adjacent high-status rooms. The larger window represents the hall, and the smaller a private chamber that was dependent on the hall.

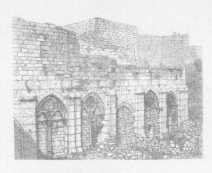

Krak des Chevaliers

The substantial size, decorative character and regular disposition of the windows at Krak des Chevaliers, in Syria, suggest a single room of generous proportions: a hall or a chapel. However, the very low position of the sills is unusual, and, in fact, they light a loggia in front of the Knight's Hall.

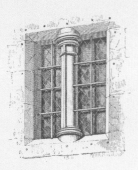

Aydon Castle

Considerations of security meant that many castle windows were barred. However, a pattern of perforations around the perimeter of this window at Aydon Castle, in Northumberland, indicates an earlier arrangement, suggesting that the present bars are not original.

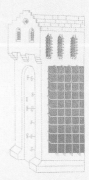

Security bars

This manuscript illustration shows the type of ironwork that was probably at Aydon originally: a series of grids fixed into the face of the window frame so that it projected beyond the elevation.

The internal shutter

Large windows were often furnished with internal wooden shutters, which fitted into a rebate cut into the window frame. Some windows were made with stone housings to receive iron bolts fitted to the shutters in order to lock the shutters when closed.

Early Medieval Windows

During the 11th and 12th centuries, when the Romanesque style of architecture was prevalent in Europe, windows were generally set beneath semi-circular arches (after the character of Roman arches) and were quite restricted in size. In castles of pronounced military character, the lower openings tend to be narrow loops so that security could be maintained. However, larger windows with greater ornamental qualities might be used at the upper levels. The more ample examples often have architectural embellishments, such as colonnettes and mouldings, and twin lights.

Château Comtal
In this 11th-century example from Carcassonne's Château Comtal, in France, the arches of the twin-light window are cut from a monolithic lintel. The central colonnette is both supportive and decorative. The internal twin wooden shutters were hung on iron pintles set in the jambs of the embrasure.

Château de Falaise

At Château de Falaise, in Normandy, France, the upper storey of the 1120s donjon is pierced by twin-light windows divided by a colonnette. The windows are flush with the external wall face. The arches themselves are constructed of voussoirs in a work of greater technical precision than the earlier example at Carcassonne.

Lillebonne Castle

A more complex form of 12th-century window construction was used at Lillebonne, in Normandy, France. Here, recessed twin lights were set beneath a flat lintel, with a semi-circular relieving arch above. An outer arch flush with the external face of the building, and springing from a pair of colonnettes, represents the vault over the window embrasure.

Oakham Castle

From the late 12th century, windows with pointed arches, such as these from the great hall of Oakham Castle, Rutland, began to increase in popularity. Dating from c.1180–90, the twin lights are flanked by colonnettes and have stylised leaf capitals set within bands of dog-tooth moulding. The arches, defined by double-roll mouldings, have tympana decorated with relief carving.

Mid-Medieval Windows

The lancet

Plain pointed windows are known as lancets. Groupings of lancets were popular during the first half of the 13th century. The west window of the great hall of Winchester Castle, in Hampshire, which dates from 1222–35, is a plain but effective grouping of three lights varying in height under a common hood mould.

By the early 13th century, pointed arches had almost entirely superseded semi-circular arches. They may be found singly or in groups. In the more prestigious apartments, in particular the great hall and sometimes the great chamber and chapel, 13th- and 14th-century pointed windows could be large and embellished with tracery, a feature that developed in complexity as the century progressed. These could be expensive items, and in rooms of lesser significance the plain rectangular loop is more likely to be found.

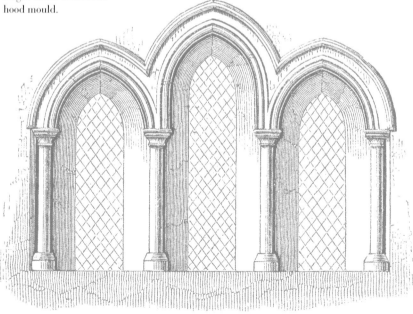

Exterior

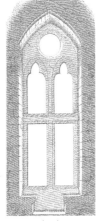

Interior

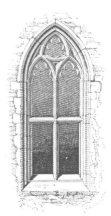

Geometric tracery

Around 1250, plate tracery gave way to bar tracery, a structural development resulting in decorative patterns of more delicate character. Early bar tracery is composed of simple geometric figures and is hence given the name 'geometric'. Geometric tracery remained popular up to c.1300. This is one of the great hall windows of Stokesay Castle, in Shropshire, of c.1280.

Plate tracery

From the early 13th century, twin- or multiple-light windows might be placed under a single hood mould, and the area between the hood mould and the window arches (the spandrel) perforated with a geometrical opening. This is known as plate tracery and was fashionable in the period c.1220–1250.

Cinquefoil-headed lights

A more urbane instance of geometric tracery, also of c.1280, can be seen at Acton Burnell Castle, in Shropshire. The cinquefoil heads of the lower lights were to become a popular feature of castle windows in the 14th century.

Late Medieval Windows

During the 14th and 15th centuries, the windows of the more significant rooms – the great hall, chapel and principal residential apartments – were given more elaborate tracery than previously. From c.1300, more complex curvilinear tracery designs succeeded the geometric patterns of the 13th century. From the mid-14th century these, in turn, were followed by the perpendicular, or rectilinear, style. However, this period was also one in which simplicity could still be found and many great hall windows are actually relatively plain in character.

The lancet
Lancet windows, a predominantly early-13th-century type in church architecture, were used in castles into the 14th century, possibly because they were comparatively plain and inexpensive. They appear at Aydon Castle, in Northumberland, in both the late-13th- and early-14th-century phases.

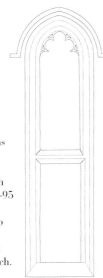

The cinquefoil head

Generally, castle windows of the late medieval period were built to simpler designs than contemporary church windows. In Bolton Castle, in North Yorkshire, the c.1377–95 chapel and great hall windows were made to a common design of a single transomed light with a cinquefoiled arch.

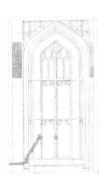

Perpendicular tracery

From the late 14th century, four-centred arches and perpendicular tracery were sometimes used. Both were employed in the great hall windows of Kenilworth Castle. These highly decorative windows are framed by mouldings and feature blind tracery around the embrasures.

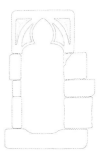

The trefoil head

Another type that was much in vogue for smaller openings during the 14th century was the trefoil-headed window. The general concept of rectangular frame, trefoil head and sunken spandrels was used widely, but individual details tend to differ from site to site.

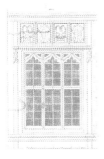

The flat lintel

Loops with flat lintels were used in less significant rooms from the 12th century onwards, but mullioned and transomed windows with flat lintels are a preserve of the later medieval period, like the example above from the 1460s.

Embrasures

Because castle walls tended to be quite thick, windows were generally framed within deep niches or embrasures. The windows themselves normally had splayed jambs designed to maximise the admittance of light, an important consideration when, for reasons of security, many castle windows could be quite narrow. Window niches often descended to, or close to, floor level in order to facilitate the opening and closing of shutters and the carrying out of any maintenance work, but also for access to fresh air, illumination and views.

The nook

The combination of enclosure and light allowed castle window embrasures to become cosy nooks within which to read, write, undertake needlework or simply converse, free from draughts and with a degree of privacy. An indication of this kind of use is the provision of integral stone seating.

Vaulting

Some window embrasures were vaulted. This treatment gave greater headroom and may have been intended to enhance the lighting qualities of the window. Here, the jambs of the embrasure are parallel, which must have simplified the construction of the vault.

The stepped sill

Stepped sills were sometimes used within embrasures to facilitate access to windows, as in this 13th-century example from Château de Coucy, in Picardy, France. The sills could also be used as seats – an alternative to lateral benches.

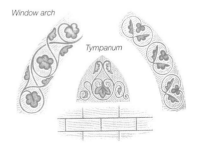

Window arch

Tympanum

Painted decoration

The Château de Coucy windows were enhanced by the application of painted decoration. The stone walls were plastered and painted in imitation of ashlar, while the arches and tympanum above the window were covered with a trailing foliate design. Both were popular 13th-century forms.

Arrow Loops

One of the principal means for the defenders of a castle to harry the enemy, without making a sortie, was to enfilade their ranks with arrows, either by bow or crossbow. The parapet of the curtain would have served as the main point of deployment in early castles, though archers here were vulnerable to retaliation from the enemy. The introduction of the arrow loop into the castle's fabric was to provide archers and crossbowmen with a relatively secure station from which to conduct their activities.

The niche
The archer's base of operations was a niche to the rear of the arrow loop, a substantial recess with room to manoeuvre, enabling the archer to get close to the loop embrasure. Like many window embrasures, these spaces were sometimes fitted with stone benches.

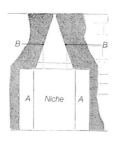

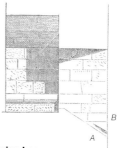

The splayed embrasure

The niche made the length of the loop in the outer wall tenable. In contrast to the straight sides of the niche (A), the loop embrasure itself was splayed (B), which allowed the archer to obtain a greater field of fire.

The sloping base

Just as the sides of the loop were splayed, the base slope (A) was splayed down towards the exterior wall (B). Here again the design was intended to assist the archer, in this case by allowing him to sight downwards to the foot of the castle.

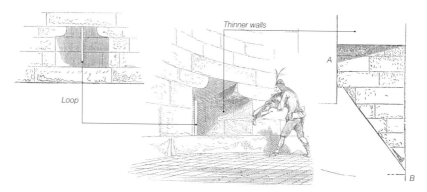

The nicheless embrasure

In castles with comparatively thin walls, the niche was unnecessary because the archer was able to get close enough to the embrasure without it. This section through the loop embrasure of a narrow-walled building (A) emphasises its manageable length in contrast to that of a thicker-walled building, where the niche is clearly needed. The much steeper pitch of the embrasure sill (B) shows that designs were varied according to circumstance.

Arrow Loops

Alternating tiers

Arrow loops were being systematically deployed by the late 12th century. At the Templar Castle of Tortosa on the Syrian coast, the upper part of the curtain contained two tiers of plain rectangular arrow loops. The loops of the lower tier alternated with those of the upper tier to obtain maximum field of fire.

At its most basic, the arrow loop is a narrow rectangular slit that allowed archers to direct their fire outside the castle while remaining concealed. It is probable that many arrow loops were intended for the deployment of crossbows, the elaborate loading of which could only be carried out with impunity if the operator were out of sight of the enemy. In use in castles from the 12th century, perhaps the arrow loop's most prolific period of use was the 13th century. However, they continued to feature in castles into the 15th century.

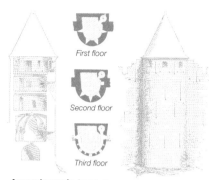

Arrow loops in towers

Methodical distribution of arrow loops was also incorporated into the designs of wall towers with a view to attaining a wide field of fire. Here, there are four tiers of loops, with a similar pattern of alternation as found in the Castle of Tortosa.

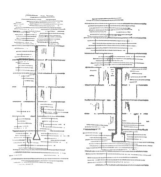

The splayed foot

Plain loops were used throughout the period, but an early innovation in design was the splayed foot, introduced to increase the archer's lateral range in firing towards the foot of the wall. These could be triangular or rectangular.

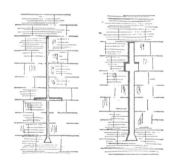

The cross slit

The other development in the evolution of the plain arrow loop was the introduction of the horizontal cross slit, probably from the early 13th century. This also improved the lateral range of fire and may have been designed specifically with the needs of the crossbowman in mind.

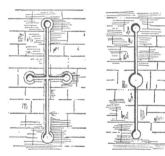

The oillet

The character of arrow slits was also subject to fashion. Round openings, known as oillets (from the French *oeil*, meaning eye), were used as terminations for arrow slits in the early 14th century. They may have had the practical purpose of increasing vision, but they were also decorative.

Gun Ports

Gun ports were being introduced into English castles in a tentative fashion from the late 14th century, probably in response to French attacks along the south coast and the threat of invasion. Their general adoption was slower in France, but they proliferated during the 15th century and became a familiar part of a castle's defensive panoply. Late medieval gun ports all appear to have been for small guns rather than for cannon. They were not so systematically deployed as arrow loops, but were concentrated in particular areas.

The oillet

A key area for gun ports was the gateway, either in the flanking towers or above the gateway itself. In this example, in which both positions are adopted, the gun ports are in the form of circular oillets, probably the earliest form of gun port.

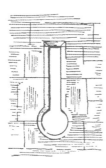

The inverted keyhole
Many early gun ports in England were of inverted keyhole type, with a circular oillet for the gun and a long sighting slit above. This form was employed c.1385 in the twin towers of the main gatehouse of Bodiam Castle, in Sussex, and in other fortifications of the period.

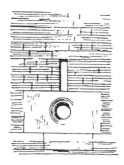

The detached sighting slit
The keyhole design also appears, c.1480, at Kirby Muxloe Castle, in Leicestershire, in a slightly different form. Here, as in other instances of this period, the sighting slit was detached from the oillet. The oillet is cut from a single block of stone and the slit is part of the surrounding brickwork.

The dumbbell
Dumbbell gun ports had a second oillet at the head of the sighting loop, either of equal size to the lower oillet or much smaller, as in this 15th-century example from the Château de Falaise, in Normandy, France.

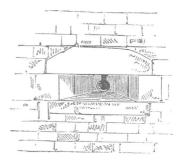

The splayed embrasure
The loops of most 14th- and 15th-century gun ports were flush with the face of the wall, but by the end of the medieval period they were being set within deep splayed embrasures to increase the field of fire.

Introduction

The underground cistern
In the Crusader states of the Middle East, a recurrent feature was the underground cistern fed by a spring. At Chastel Blanc, in Syria, a cistern beneath the donjon could be tapped from a trap in the ground floor, and there was a well outside the door of the tower.

Quite apart from being essential to withstanding a siege, a reliable water supply was vital to the everyday life of a castle, for drinking, washing, cooking, brewing and cleaning. Every permanent castle, therefore, had at least one well. Some were situated within the courtyard, while others might be housed in more secure accommodation such as a tower. Arrangements might also be made for storing water, a particularly important consideration in regions such as the Middle East where rainfall was infrequent.

The well

In western Europe the well was usually the main source of water. Most castle wells are now no more than a hole in the ground, but they would have had a superstructure housing a windlass by which the water was drawn.

Alnwick Castle

Although most wells were of a utilitarian nature, some had a decidedly architectural character. A rare 14th-century survival at Alnwick Castle, in Northumberland, has the form of a three-bay arcade recessed beneath a moulded arch.

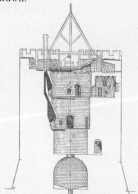

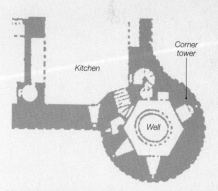

Corner tower

Kitchen

Well

The well in the great tower

Sometimes wells were accommodated in the great tower, as at Conisbrough Castle, in South Yorkshire. The well was set within the floor of the vaulted basement, and was drawn from first-floor level via a trap.

The well chamber (plan)

Some internal wells were housed in special chambers in areas that required ready access to water. At Bodiam Castle, in Sussex, the well chamber was in the basement of a corner tower, next to the kitchens.

Lavers, Sinks & Drains

The laver

Lavers could be quite ornate features that enhanced the decorative quality of their surroundings. This delicate example is in the first-floor hall of the tower house of Dacre Castle, in Cumbria. The design is indistinguishable from that of a piscina in this case, but its context suggests that it was intended as a laver.

Arrangements for the use and disposal of water were often built into the fabric of castles. Washing of hands was an important ritual before dining, and built-in washing facilities were sometimes provided in the form of lavers – niches containing sinks with a drain – that discharged outside the castle wall. Drains are also found in service areas associated with food preparation. A similar feature is the urinal, which worked on the same principle, but which is sometimes distinguishable from the laver by having less room for manoeuvre. No doubt, one feature sometimes served both purposes.

The latrine sink

Sinks are sometimes found in association with latrines, usually within the mural passage approach, and often beneath a window. One such exists in a residential chamber at Warwick Castle, in Warwickshire. Here, the latrine is entered from a window embrasure and the laver is situated under the window.

The kitchen sink

The sink could be a great convenience in a kitchen, where water was much in use for cooking and cleaning, and had to be disposed of once used. The projecting basin of this one in the early 14th-century kitchen of Aydon Castle, in Northumberland, indicates its function as a sink rather than simply a drain.

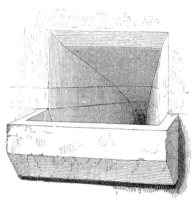

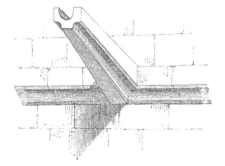

The drainage spout

Internal drains usually terminated on the exterior wall in spouts or gargoyles, though unlike ecclesiastical gargoyles they were seldom decorated. In interpreting a building from the exterior, such features can be useful as evidence of internal layout and room function.

Latrines

The corbelled latrine
Latrines were often housed in projections, or turrets, corbelled out from the wall face so that the waste was deposited outside the castle, and unpleasant smells were dissipated. In this example from Château Landsberg, in Alsace, France, the seat consists of a stone slab with a hole cut through it. Being entirely outside the castle wall, it was vulnerable, but the front of the opening is protected from missiles by a suspended stone.

In a large building like a castle, which was designed for a considerable number of inhabitants, there was often a liberal provision of latrines. The presence of a latrine can be a useful indication that the room it served was designed for a residential function. One of the main factors affecting the design of latrines was the need for regular cleaning. Hence they were nearly always situated on or within external walls so that the waste could be collected and disposed of with the minimum of inconvenience.

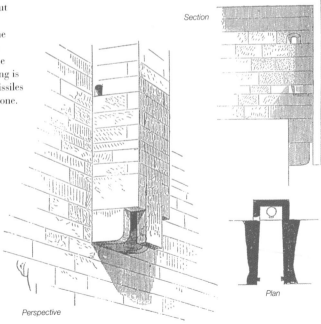

Section

Perspective

Plan

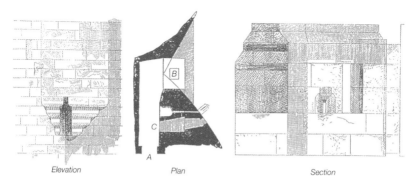

Elevation *Plan* *Section*

Château de Coucy

The 13th-century latrines at Château de Coucy, in Picardy, France, were also corbelled. Situated in the angles between the curtain and the rounded towers, they needed multiple tiers of corbelling to give the projection required. The latrines were accessible from stair landings (A) between the towers and from adjacent domestic ranges. They consisted of passage-like mural chambers with the seat (B) at the far end spanning the angle between tower and curtain. The chamber was lit by a window (C) and next to it was the urinal with a mural drain terminating in an external spout, discharging beyond the castle wall.

The latrine turret

The enclosed projection, or turret, was a development of corbelled latrine projections. This contained the sewage and allowed for its more effective disposal. At Wressle Castle, in East Yorkshire, such turrets are situated in the angle between the corner towers and adjacent residential ranges. These latrine turrets date from c.1390.

Latrine Tower

Sometimes there was a need or desire to concentrate latrines in one area. A recurrent feature of the great monastic castles of the Teutonic Knights in north-east Europe, which housed large communities of warriors, was the latrine tower, or dansker. This facility, which was placed over a watercourse, was detached from the main body of the castle and approached by a viaduct. In secular castles, where the household was not arranged in such uncompromising fashion, towers devoted entirely to latrines are unusual, although they were occasionally adopted.

Langley Castle

An example of a secular latrine tower can be found at the mid-14th-century tower house of Langley Castle, in Northumberland. One of the four projecting corner towers contains three storeys of communal latrines. Each latrine was contained within an arched recess and all discharged into a common pit at ground-floor level, which was flushed by a stream. The second and third tiers are set back from the one below so that all have an unimpeded drop to the pit.

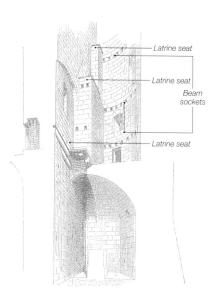

Latrine seat

Latrine seat

Beam
sockets

Latrine seat

Château de Pierrefonds

A different system, of c.1400,
was implemented at Château de
Pierrefonds, near Paris. Here, the
lowest storey of the latrine tower
contained the pit. Above this were
three storeys of communal latrines
staggered from one side of the
tower to the other. The beam
sockets indicate the positions of the floors.

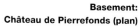

Basement:
Château de Pierrefonds (plan)

An air vent was incorporated in the
vaulted basement (A), and a channel
below the latrine shafts extended
through the wall (B) to
facilitate extraction of waste.

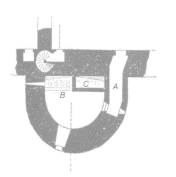

Ground-floor:
Château de Pierrefonds (plan)

Above the basement was the ground
storey (courtyard level). As on the
other storeys, the latrine tower was
entered via a long mural passage (A).
Four seats (B) were recessed and
sited next to the latrine shaft
extending from the upper storey (C).

Introduction

The open hearth

The open hearth was a feature of very ancient origin. It was often used to heat the great hall – originally the communal dining room of a great house. The hearth was formed by a metalled surface of stone or tile and surrounded by a kerb, as in the great hall of Penshurst Place, in Kent.

While castles often seem spartan residences, there is ample evidence, in the form of fireplaces and chimneys, to show that serious attention was paid to the provision of heating. In addition to being functional conveniences, however, a fireplace was often the main focus of a room, and the chimney added to the interest of a castle's roofline. Given these considerations, both were objects of embellishment, and, in common with other architectural details, were subject to stylistic change over the centuries. In consequence, both can provide useful dating evidence.

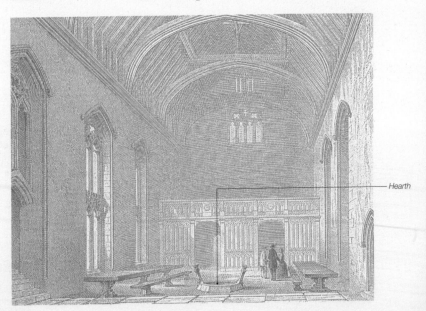

— Hearth

The louvre

The smoke from an open hearth was dispersed via a louvre, which was usually a timber-framed structure on the roof. While practical, louvres could be quite elaborate decorative constructions. Few survive. The example shown here is a copy of the late-14th-century louvre of Westminster Hall, in London.

The smoke vent

The smoke from early wall fireplaces was dispersed by flues. These extended through the wall to the exterior face, where they terminated in rectangular vents. In this c.1130 example, in the keep of Colchester Castle, in Essex, the vents are placed to either side of a buttress to give some protection from the wind.

The lodging chimney

During the late Middle Ages, castle lodgings for individuals proliferated in order to accommodate the enlarged retinues of great magnates. Many of these lodgings were provided with their own fireplaces, sometimes served by external chimney stacks. In these circumstances, the external evidence alone may identify a lodging range.

Early Medieval Fireplaces

Fireplaces were in use in castles from the 11th century at the latest. A characteristic of early fireplaces is that they were set within deep mural recesses to lessen the possibility of smoke escaping into the room rather than up the chimney. Later 12th-century fireplaces were set beneath projecting canopies or hoods, a device that allowed the hearths to be set less deeply, and which increased the effectiveness of the fire by bringing it further into the room, thereby diminishing heat loss.

Colchester Castle
Early castle fireplaces were often arched, as in this 1080s example in Colchester Castle, in Essex. Roman tiles were used to frame its opening and line its semi-circular back. The herringbone fashion continued into the late medieval period.

Rochester Castle

Semi-circular arched fireplaces continued into the 12th century, and sometimes reflect the form of door and window openings of that period. This c.1130 example in the keep of Rochester Castle, in Kent, has shafts with bases and capitals from which the moulded arch springs. Like other early Norman fireplaces, the plan of the flue is semi-circular.

Château de Veauce

In 12th-century fireplaces, the segmental arch offered an alternative to the semi-circular arch, as in the Château de Veauce in the Auvergne, France. As at Rochester Castle, the moulded arch springs from engaged shafts. The fireplace breaks forward from the face of the wall and is hooded, so the wall is not so deeply recessed.

The joggled lintel

From the late 12th century, hooded fireplaces were usual. At Conisbrough Castle, in South Yorkshire, two examples are to be found on the upper floors of the keep, which dates from c.1190. Each has a joggled lintel, a jointing technique that obviated the need for a large stone lintel.

Late Medieval Fireplaces

The hooded fireplace, which was the dominant type in the 13th century, continued into the 14th. Although it diminished in popularity in late-14th-century England, its use continued in other countries, including France and Scotland. In 14th-century England, the corbelled lintel became a popular alternative to the hood, and fireplaces with low arches were also in use. With the expansion of high-quality accommodation and greater attention to comfort that characterised late medieval castles, good fireplaces proliferated.

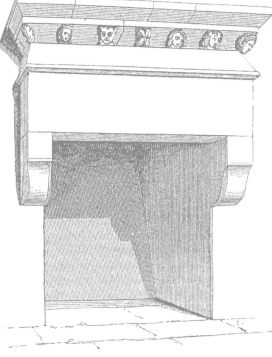

The lintel corbel

In the 14th century, the lintel corbel became a popular alternative to the shafts that were such a feature of 13th-century fireplaces. Aydon Castle, in Northumberland, has one fireplace with ogee-curved corbels supporting a monolithic lintel and a mantelpiece decorated with carved heads.

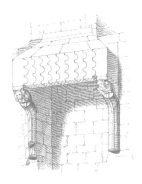

The sculptured corbel
Lintel corbels might serve as locations for sculptural embellishment, as in this 14th-century fireplace at Edlingham Castle, in Northumberland. An elaborate joggled lintel is carried on sculptured corbels that terminate in a pair of curving shafts.

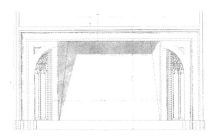

The perpendicular style
The fireplace of the great hall of Kenilworth Castle, in Warwickshire, is part of an important architectural scheme in the perpendicular style carried out in the 1370s. The splayed jambs are in the form of traceried panels framed by bold roll mouldings, which are configured beneath the lintel to imitate the corbels of a Caernarfon arch.

Borthwick Castle
A fireplace might be used to create an architectural focus, as in the great hall of the 1430 tower house of Borthwick Castle, in Scotland. The massive construction of the fireplace and the tall 'obelisk' of the hood dominate the upper end of the hall.

The Tudor arch
A frieze of quatrefoil panels and a low Tudor arch with decorated sunken spandrels were popular forms of fireplace in the 15th and early 16th centuries. This example at Thornbury Castle, in Gloucestershire, dates from c.1520.

Chimneys

It wasn't until the mid-12th century that chimneys as we know them came into existence. However, once they had been established, what had begun as a purely practical expedient took on an ornamental role and was to make a significant contribution to the profile of the castle. This aspect of castle architecture is no longer much in evidence, but examples that do survive give an impression of the architectural possibilities that might be exacted from a practical feature.

The capped chimney with side vents

In many early medieval chimneys, smoke escaped through vents in the side of the shaft and the top was fitted with a conical cap. This type was in existence by the mid-12th century. A late-13th-century example at Aydon Castle, in Northumberland, is external to the building and does not rise above the parapet.

The octagonal chimney

Octagonal chimney stacks became fashionable in the early 14th century. An example survives at Grosmont Castle in Wales. In each of the eight faces, a trefoil-arched side vent is set beneath a miniature gable. Rising above the gables is a stumpy cap with decorative cresting.

The cylindrical chimney

Where there are several fireplaces on the same wall of a building, there might be a cluster of chimney stacks at roof level. On the late-13th-century great tower of Stokesay Castle, in Shropshire, there are two cylindrical stacks with moulded rims. Cylindrical chimney stacks appeared from the mid-12th century onwards.

The crenellated cap

In the early 14th century, chimneys with crenellated caps came into vogue. A c.1345 example at Maxstoke Castle, in Warwickshire, is unusual in having two tiers of crenellation instead of the more usual one. The octagonal-sectioned form of this chimney is in sympathy with the octagonal corner towers of the castle.

The iron crown

The existence of iron chimney cappings is attested in France, although they rarely survive. An exception is at the late-14th-century Château de Sully-sur-Loire, in France. At the gable end of the great hall, an oval-sectioned stone chimney stack is fitted with an iron crown terminating in fleur-de-lys finials.

Introduction

An important aspect of castle design was how people would circulate between different parts of the building. This was to weigh more heavily in the late medieval period as castle planning became more complex. The staircase was an essential element in providing rational and efficient lines of communication, though it is not always accorded the attention it deserves. Achieving an economy of materials, construction technique and space were all considerations that affected the development of the staircase.

The supporting arch

A castle invariably required a staircase to reach the allure. Where this needed to be a substantial construction, it was even more necessary to practise economy of materials. In this instance, instead of building on a solid base, the steps are supported on two demi-arches, a technological solution typical of the Gothic period.

The covered staircase

Where the great hall was at first-floor level, it might be approached by an external, often roofed, staircase. Surviving grooves in the masonry indicate that at Aydon Castle, in Northumberland, the staircase to the hall initially rose to a porch. This was later replaced by a roof that extended over most of the staircase.

The turret staircase

To ensure that external stairs ascending the corner bartizans of a tower did not encroach on the roof, it was usual to build them on top of the perimeter walls. In some cases, however, this wasn't possible. Here the solution was to build the steps into the wall of the bartizan (they were later underbuilt).

Carlisle Castle

Castle staircases are mostly plain and functional. Occasionally, there is an unusual degree of embellishment that suggests a special importance. One of the few surviving vestiges of the royal apartments of Carlisle Castle, in Cumbria, is the 14th-century polygonal stair turret in the inner bailey, which is ornamented with blind tracery.

Spiral Stairs

Colchester Castle
Although spiral
staircases could be
compact, and sometimes
restricted, there was
no reason why they
could not be spacious.
An example is the
11th-century staircase
in the keep of Colchester
Castle, in Essex. Because
it was sited in a turret
rather than within the
thickness of a wall,
it could be built to
stately proportions.

The most commonly used type of staircase in castles
was the spiral, probably owing to its compact,
economical and flexible nature. It has often been said
that spiral staircases in castles were designed with a
clockwise thread so that a defender of the castle
(descending) would have an advantage over an
attacker (ascending) in that his sword (right) arm
would be free. Recent research has indicated that there
is no good reason to suppose this to be true; both
clockwise and anticlockwise threads have been recorded.

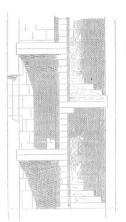

The umbrella vault (right)

Some spiral staircases ended in a flat stone roof supported by the stair newel while others, like this example in the donjon of Warkworth Castle, in Northumberland, were vaulted. This particular form, known as an umbrella vault, was prevalent in northern England during the 14th century.

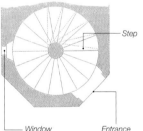

Step

Window — Entrance

The one-piece tread (above)

The introduction of the one-piece tread around the end of the 12th century revolutionised the construction of spiral staircases. Cut from a single slab of stone, each step incorporated a section of newel post. Construction was greatly simplified and the need for vaulting obviated.

The spiralling vault (left)

Spiral staircases of the 11th and 12th centuries were vaulted either in a mortar mix or in stone. The initial steps were raised on a solid base with subsequent steps raised on top of the spiralling vaults. The central newel post and the wall of the stairwell acted as abutments for the vault.

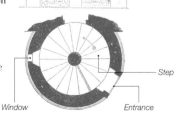

Step

Window — Entrance

Straight Stairs

Although the spiral staircase is the type most associated with castles, straight staircases were also common. Often built within the thickness of a wall, they were simpler to build than the spiral and, depending on the circumstances, could sometimes create a line of communication more conveniently. The approach to the upper-storey main entrance of a great tower could be better controlled if it was in the form of a straight staircase, and in cylindrical great towers the 'straight' mural staircase was often used in spiral fashion to climb between storeys.

Castle Rising

While most castle staircases are of the severely practical kind, there were many instances of them being used to create an impression of grandeur. Such was the case at Castle Rising, in Norfolk. The main approach to the interior of the 12th-century keep is in the form of a ceremonial staircase of grand proportions.

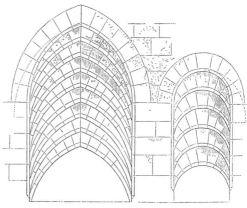

The arched staircase (above)

The builders of straight mural staircases faced the problem of how to manage the thrust emitted by the solid walling above it. The most structurally sound solution for wide staircases was to cover them with an ascending series of arches springing from the same height relative to the steps.

The corbelled ceiling (below)

In roofing a narrow mural staircase, it was safe to adopt a technically simpler and more cost-effective alternative to vaulting – a series of lintels supported on corbels. While these did not have the strength of arches, they were perfectly adequate for a space of limited span.

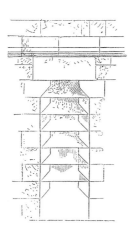

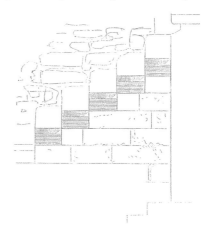

Glossary

ALLURE
The circulatory path around the top of a wall behind the parapet, used as a fighting platform. Also known as a wall walk.

APSE
A projecting part of a building, usually semi-circular in plan and vaulted.

ARROW LOOP
A narrow vertical opening with splayed sides through which arrows were fired by the defenders of a castle.

ASHLAR
Masonry comprising accurately squared blocks laid in finely jointed horizontal courses.

BAILEY
The courtyard of a castle enclosed by a curtain wall or palisade.

BARBICAN
An additional castle defence built in front of the gatehouse.

BARTIZAN
A small, overhanging turret usually built at an angle and used in defence and/or as an ornament.

BASTION
The external projection of a castle wall, providing a wide-angled defensive position for the building. Also known as a bulwark.

BATTER
The splayed base of a wall added to enhance the castle's defensive capabilities.

BATTLEMENTS
See Crenellations.

BELFRY
A mobile timber siege tower used in an attack on a castle.

BELL TOWER
A type of church tower built to house bells.

BLIND ARCADE
Arches that have no openings, which are added to the surface of a wall as decoration.

BOSS
A projection from a wall, roof or other surface.

BOSSED MASONRY
Stone blocks with bosses projecting from the face.

BULWARK
See Bastion.

BURG
The term for castle used in several Germanic languages.

BUTTRESS
The localised thickening of, or projection from, the wall of a building to strengthen or shore.

CAPITAL
The feature at the top of a column. It broadens the area of the column's supporting surface, as well as adding decoration.

CASTELLATED
See Crenellated.

CHASTEL
Old French term for castle.

CHÂTEAU
The French term for manor house or castle.

CHEMISE
The subsidiary wall surrounding a taller building, usually a tower. Also known as a mantlet.

CITADEL
A castle-like fortress within a walled town.

CONCENTRIC CASTLE
A castle with two concentric circuits of curtain wall.

COPING
The capping stones of a wall.

CORBEL
Projecting blocks of stone built into a wall to bear a downward weight. Used to support parapets, hoardings, machicolations and turrets.

CRENEL
The gap between the raised sections of stonework of a crenellated parapet. Also known as an embrasure.

CRENELLATED
Fortified by being provided with crenellations.

CRENELLATIONS
A defendable parapet in raised sections alternating with gaps.

CRUSADES
The series of Holy Wars launched by the Christian states of Europe against the Islamic states in Asia Minor and the Levant.

CURTAIN WALL
The main wall enclosing a castle.

DONJON
See Keep.

DRAWBRIDGE
The bridge across a moat in front of an entrance. A drawbridge could be withdrawn or raised to hinder access.

DRUM TOWER
A rounded projecting wall tower.

EARTHWORKS
Ditches, banks, mottes and other artificial earthen constructions used in castle building.

EMBRASURE
The splayed opening in a castle wall for a window. Also used as an alternative name for crenel.

ENCEINTE
A continuous ring of fortifications surrounding a town or castle.

ENCLOSURE CASTLE
A keepless castle.

ENFILADE
To discharge guns or arrows in an uninterrupted line of fire.

ESCALADE
To scale defensive walls or ramparts, usually by ladders.

FOREBUILDING
The projection from the castle keep containing and protecting the entrance.

GALLERY
A raised and covered walkway.

GARDEROBE
Medieval term for lavatory.

GATEHOUSE
A fortified structure containing the gateway to a castle.

GOTHIC
Architectural style that originated in France in the late medieval period and was adopted across Europe. It is predominantly seen in churches and cathedrals, but was also used for castles, halls, universities and other important public buildings. The Gothic style is characterised by its use of pointed arches and vaulting, and an interest in the possibilities of light. Interest in the Gothic style was revived during the 18th and 19th centuries.

GREAT HALL
The principal room of a medieval great house, used as a communal dining room.

GREAT TOWER
See Keep.

GUN PORT
The opening in a castle wall designed for firing guns through.

HALL KEEP
A keep that is low in proportion to its ground plan.

HOARDINGS
Temporary or permanent overhanging wooden galleries erected at the top of a castle wall providing defensive positions.

JAMB
An upright piece of material forming the side of an opening, such as a door, window or fireplace.

KEEP
The principal tower within a castle. Also known as a donjon or great tower.

KREMLIN
The citadel of a Russian city.

LINTEL
A horizontal piece of material that spans and usually carries the load above an opening, such as a window or door.

MACHICOLATIONS
Projecting stone galleries at the head of a wall with slots in the base through which projectiles could be dropped.

MANGONEL
A stone-throwing engine operated on the principle of torsion.

MANTLET
See Chemise.

MEDIEVAL
Period of European history between the fall of the Roman Empire and the Renaissance. Exact definitions of the dates vary, but for the purposes of this book, the medieval era refers to the period between the early 12th century and the mid-16th century.

MERLONS
The raised sections of a crenellated wall.

MIDDLE AGES
Term used synonymously with medieval.

MOAT
A deep, broad ditch encircling a castle sometimes filled with water.

Glossary

MOTTE
A mound used as a base for a tower, palisade and other buildings.

MURDER HOLES
Openings in a ceiling or floor, usually over a gateway, either for directing missiles through or as conduits for water to dowse fires.

OILLET
A circular opening used as a termination for an arrow loop, or, on its own, as a gun loop.

OUTWORK
Minor fortification built outside the main defensive position.

PALISADE
A defensive fence of timber stakes enclosing a castle bailey.

PARAPET
The stone screen at the head of a wall protecting the allure.

PETRARIE
Stone-throwing engines.

PINTLE
A pin or bolt used as part of a pivot or hinge.

PORTCULLIS
Heavy grilled gate operated on a vertical plane between grooves in the flanking stonework.

POSTERN
A minor gateway additional to the main gateway.

RAM
Battering ram comprising a thick spar with reinforced head. Used to batter down gates and other timber fortifications.

RAVELIN
A pointed fortification designed to split an attacking force.

REVETMENT
A wall used to shore up a bank of earth.

RINGWORK
The name given to the earthwork remains of a timber enclosure castle.

RUSTICATED MASONRY
See Bossed Masonry.

SALLY PORT
Type of postern used by the defenders of a castle to launch attacks on the enemy.

SHELL KEEP
The stone wall encircling the top of a motte.

SIEGE
Surrounding of a castle by an armed force to cut off its supplies of food and water and force the occupants to comply with their demands or to surrender.

SIEGE ENGINE
A device designed for the purpose of breaking through a castle's defences.

SLIGHTING
Deliberate destruction of fortifications in order to render them indefensible.

SOLAR
A residential room positioned on an upper storey within a medieval house.

SPANDREL
The space between two arches or between an arch and a rectangular enclosure.

TALUS
Splayed base of a wall rising to a greater height than a batter.

TENSHUKAKU
The keep of a Japanese castle.

TRACERY
Pattern of open stonework or woodwork in a Gothic window.

TORRE
Term for tower used in Spanish, Italian and Portuguese.

TREBUCHET
A siege engine operated on the principle of counterweight.

TURRETS
Small towers projecting from a wall.

VOUSSOIRS
A wedge-shaped element used in the construction of an arch or vault.

WALL WALK
See Allure.

WATER CHUTE
An inclined channel built into the wall of a castle through which water could be poured to dowse fires.

YAMASHIRO
Japanese mountaintop castle.

Resources

Books

Creighton, Oliver. *Castles and Landscapes: Power, Community and Fortification in Medieval England*. Sheffield: Equinox, 2005.

Creighton, Oliver. *Early European Castles: Aristocracy and Authority, AD 800–1200*. London: Bristol Classical Press, 2012.

Emery, Anthony. *Greater Medieval Houses of England and Wales*, 3 volumes. Cambridge: Cambridge University Press, 1996–2006.

Goodall, John. *The English Castle 1066–1650*. Newhaven and London: Yale University Press, 2011.

Higham, Robert And Barker, Philip. *Timber Castles*. London: Batsford, 1992.

Impey, Edward. *The White Tower*. Newhaven and London: Yale University Press, 2008.

Kennedy, Hugh. *Crusader Castles*. Cambridge: Cambridge University Press, 1994.

Kenyon, John. *Medieval Fortifications*. London and New York: Continuum, 2005

Liddiard, Robert. *Castles in Context: Power Symbolism and Landscape, 1066 to 1500*. Macclesfield: Windgather Press, 2005.

Mcneill, Tom. *Castles*. London: Batsford, 2006.

Mesqui, Jean. *Châteaux et Enceintes de la France Médiévale: De la défense à la résidence*, 2 volumes. Paris: Picard, 1991–1993.

Mesqui, Jean. *Châteux Forts et Fortifications en France*. Paris: Flammarion, 1997.

Web sites

www.casteland.com
Gazetteer of castle sites in France.

www.castlesofspain.co.uk
Information on Spanish castles.

www.castlestudiesgroup.org.uk
Web site of the Castle Studies Group in the UK.

www.consorziocastelli.it
Gazetteer of castles in Italy.

www.gatehouse-gazetteer.info
Gazetteer of castle sites in England and Wales.

Gazetteer

Index

Index

Acknowledgements

Author Acknowledgements

My thanks are extended to my contacts at the Ivy Press, notably Stephanie Evans, Caroline Earle and Jane Roe, and their colleagues, for their diligence and skill in bringing this work together. I am grateful also to the 19th-century pioneers, particularly Eugène E. Viollet-le-Duc, in France, and Thomas H. Turner and John H. Parker, in England, from whose works many of these illustrations were taken, and to the more recent scholars and authors the results of whose research has enriched this book.

A special debt of gratitude is owed to my wife Anne for her assistance, understanding and reassuring presence.

The publisher would like to thank the following individuals and organisations for their kind permission to reproduce the images in this book. Every effort has been made to acknowledge the pictures, however we apologise if there are any unintentional omissions.

Clipart Images/Clipart.com: 89BR.
Dover Publications Inc./Castles: Their Construction and History by Sidney Toy: 33, 43TL, 46, 47, 49T, 75, 77, 85, 97, 107, 113, 119, 123, 127, 144, 145, 159, 165, 169, 173, 177, 200, 201, 221, 223.
Fotolia/Morphart Creation: 87BL.
Getty Images/Hulton Archive: 7, 42; Universal Images Group: 47BL.
Adam Hook: 68, 72.
Alamy/Lebrecht Music and Arts Photo Library: 14.
Library of Congress: 50.
Mary Evans Picture Library/BeBa/Iberfoto: 26.
Shutterstock/Morphart Creation: 20, 34, 91BL.; Hein Nouwens: 23, 37, 44, 91BR.
Peter Scolefield: 45.
Thinkstock/Getty Images: 22.
Steven Turnbull: 23BL.

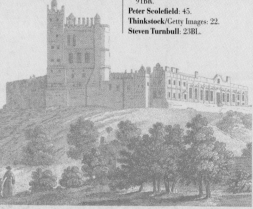